DAY HIKES AROUND
BOZEMAN
MONTANA

INCLUDING THE GALLATIN
CANYON AND PARADISE VALLEY

by Robert Stone

Day Hike Books, Inc.
RED LODGE, MONTANA

Published by Day Hike Books, Inc.
P.O. Box 865
Red Lodge, Montana 59068

Distributed by The Globe Pequot Press
246 Goose Lane
P.O. Box 480
Guilford, CT 06437-0480
800-243-0495 (direct order) · 800-820-2329 (fax order)
www.globe-pequot.com

Photographs by Robert Stone
Design by Paula Doherty

The author has made every attempt to provide accurate
information in this book. However, trail routes and features may
change—please use common sense and forethought, and be mindful
of your own capabilities. Let this book guide you, but be aware
that each hiker assumes responsibility for their own safety.
The author and publisher do not assume any responsibility for loss,
damage or injury caused through the use of this book.

Cover photo: Shower Creek along the
Hyalite Creek Trail — Hike 30.
Back cover photo: Hyalite Lake — Hike 30.

Table of Contents

THE HIKES

Bridger Mountains — West Side

Bridger Mountains — East Side

In and Around Bozeman

Yellowstone National Park from the Gallatin

Bear Canyon

Paradise Valley

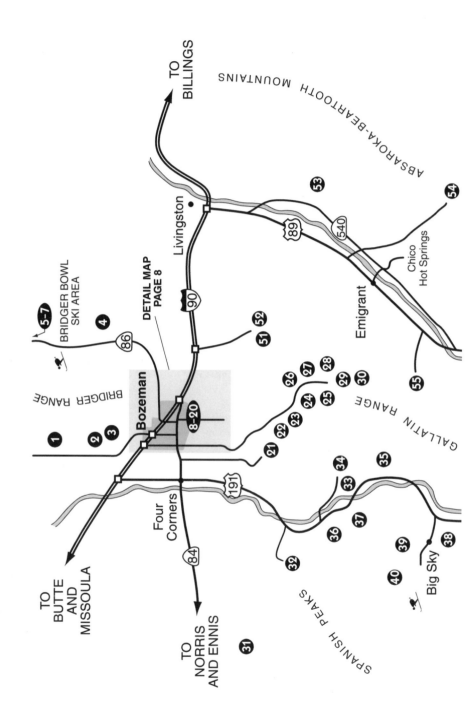

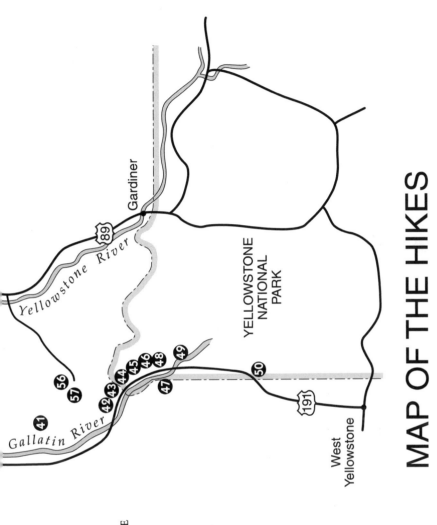

MAP OF THE HIKES

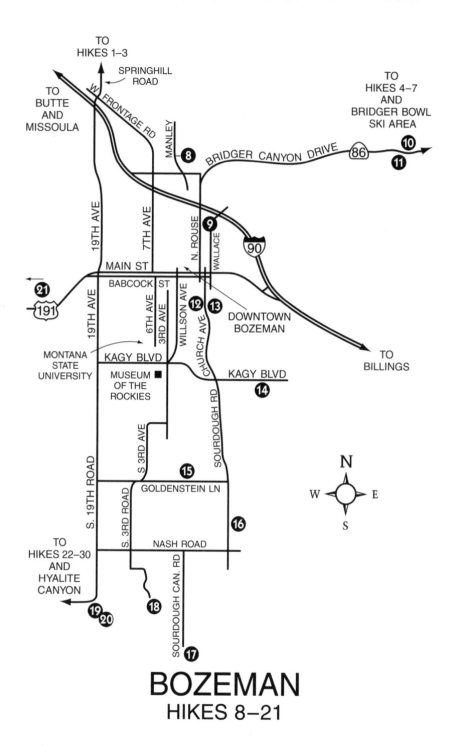

BOZEMAN
HIKES 8–21

About Bozeman and the Hikes

Bozeman, Montana, is an active, thriving town dating back to the 1880s. It is rich in character, history and landscape. There are eight historical districts, a wide variety of museums, art galleries, musical events, and is home to Montana State University. Surrounded by extraordinary wilderness, Bozeman is a gateway city to the Gallatin National Forest and Yellowstone National Park.

The Gallatin National Forest, part of the Greater Yellowstone Area, encompasses 1.7 million acres and contains some of the highest mountains in Montana. It is comprised of six mountain ranges — the Absaroka, Beartooth, Bridger, Crazy, Gallatin and Madison Ranges. Many peaks rise above 10,000 feet. The sheer grandeur of this national forest includes the protected 259,000-acre Lee Metcalf Wilderness and the 945,000-acre Absaroka-Beartooth Wilderness. The forest also contains the headwaters to the Boulder, Gallatin and Madison Rivers, plus hundreds of miles of creeks and tributaries. Many of the rivers have a blue-ribbon rating for fishing. The Gallatin National Forest has an abundance of wildlife, including black and grizzly bear, moose, elk, mountain lions, big horn sheep, mountain goats and deer. Whether fishing, kayaking, rafting, mountain climbing, horse-back riding, camping, biking, backpacking or hiking, this area has endless opportunities for outdoor recreation.

There are two main routes to many of the hikes in this book — Highway 191 and Highway 89. Highway 191 snakes south through the Gallatin Canyon along the Gallatin River. The highway connects Bozeman with Big Sky, a year-round resort community, and West Yellowstone, the west entrance to Yellowstone National Park. The Gallatin River and Highway 191 travel through two mountain ranges. To the west is the Madison Range, which includes the Lee Metcalf Wilderness and Spanish Peaks. To the east is the Gallatin Range, which includes the Hyalite Drainage. Hikes 32—50 are accessed through the Gallatin Valley and river drainage.

The rugged 78,000-acre Spanish Peaks Wilderness Area, part of the Lee Metcalf Wilderness, is located north of Big Sky and west of Highway 191. The steep Spanish Peaks contain some of the oldest rocks in North America. The 3-billion year old metamorphic rocks were sculpted by glaciers, wind and water. Within the area are 25 peaks rising above 10,000 feet, including Gallatin Peak at 11,015 feet. Below the peaks are wide subalpine meadows, forested valleys and more than 175 lakes. A web of trails interconnect this gorgeous area.

The 34,000-acre Hyalite Drainage is a stunning mountain valley that sits between the Gallatin Canyon and Paradise Valley south of Bozeman. This drainage is a popular recreational area with a large reservoir built in the 1940s as its centerpiece. The reservoir has a holding capacity of 8,000 acre feet of water. Its coves and caves, plus easily accessible piers, offer great trout fishing spots. Hyalite Reservoir is used for drinking water for the city of Bozeman and to irrigate the Gallatin Valley. The Hyalite Drainage Recreational Area is surrounded by 10,000-foot mountain peaks and includes a large variety of biking and hiking trails, creeks, streams, lakes and numerous waterfalls. Hikes 22—30 lie in the Hyalite Canyon and Reservoir area.

Highway 89 begins about 20 miles east of Bozeman at Livingston. The highway parallels the Yellowstone River, the largest free-flowing river in the lower 48 states, through Paradise Valley. The 53-mile stretch connects Livingston with the towns of Pray, Emigrant and Gardiner to the north entrance of Yellowstone National Park. Highway 89 is flanked by the Gallatin Range on the west and the Absaroka Range on the east. Hikes 53—57 are found in and around Paradise Valley.

To the north of Bozeman lies the Bridger Range, home to the Bridger Mountains National Recreation Trail and Bridger Bowl Ski Area. Many recreational opportunities can be found in this scenic mountain range because of its close proximity to

Bozeman, yet this area retains its remoteness. Hikes 1—7 are found among the Bridgers.

This book focuses on 57 hikes of various lengths around Bozeman and in these surrounding mountain ranges and valleys. The hikes range from easy to moderately strenuous and have been chosen for their scenery, variety and ability to be hiked within the day. An overall map of the 57 hikes is found on the previous pages. Each hike has a summary of its highlights, driving and hiking directions, plus an adjoining map.

If you wish to extend your hike further into the back-country, many of the trails are detailed on an assortment of commercial maps. These include the U.S. Geological Survey topographical maps and the U.S. Forest Service Gallatin National Forest maps. Relevant maps are listed with each hike and can be purchased at most area sporting goods stores.

Be sure to wear supportive, comfortable hiking shoes and be prepared for inclement weather. The elevation for these hikes can be as high as 10,000 feet. At this altitude the air can be cool. Afternoon thundershowers are common throughout the summer. Be prepared for unpredictable weather by wearing layered clothing and packing a warm hat. A rain poncho, sunscreen, mosquito repellent and drinking water are highly recommended.

Enjoy your hike as you discover Bozeman and the beautiful valleys and forests that surround this mountain community.

Notes:

A bear bell is advised to alert bears of your presence. The Gallatin National Forest has both black and grizzly bears. Surprising them is not safe. Hike with a friend or group if at all possible.

The "Main Street to the Mountains" trails in Bozeman are built and maintained by the Gallatin Valley Land Trust. Their efforts and accomplishments are largely due to volunteer labor, donations and grants. They can be reached at (406) 587-8404.

Hike 1
Truman Gulch Trail

Hiking distance: 4 miles round trip
Hiking time: 2 hours
Elevation gain: 750 feet
Maps: U.S.G.S. Saddle Peak
       U.S.F.S. Gallatin National Forest West Half or East Half

Summary of hike: Hikes 1—7 are found in the Bridger Mountains, a beautiful range which runs north and south to the north of Bozeman. The Truman Gulch Trail parallels the Truman Gulch drainage up canyon to the Bridger National Recreation Trail. The trail is surrounded by forested rolling mountains and beautiful views. The hike stays close to the trickling sound of the stream and has several stream crossings.

Driving directions: From I-90 and the 7th Avenue overpass, drive 2 miles north on 7th Avenue, which becomes West Frontage Road, to Springhill Road. Turn right (north) and continue 8.5 miles to Springhill Community Road on the right. There is a sign for Truman Gulch. Turn right and continue 1.6 miles to Walker Road. The Springhill Church is on this corner. Turn right and drive 1.1 mile to Forswell Road and turn left. Continue 3 miles to the trailhead parking area at road's end.

Hiking directions: From the parking area, the wide trail heads east into the canyon and past a horse gate. At 0.2 miles is a stream crossing. Continue gradually uphill through the forest. There are two more stream crossings at 1.8 miles. As you near 2 miles, the trail opens up to views of the surrounding mountains. There are various converging drainages and a stream crossing. This is our turnaround spot. Return along the same trail.

    To hike further, the Truman Gulch Trail climbs 0.6 miles steeply out of the valley to a junction with the Bridger Mountains National Recreation Trail. To the south, the trail connects with Middle Cottonwood Creek (Hike 2).

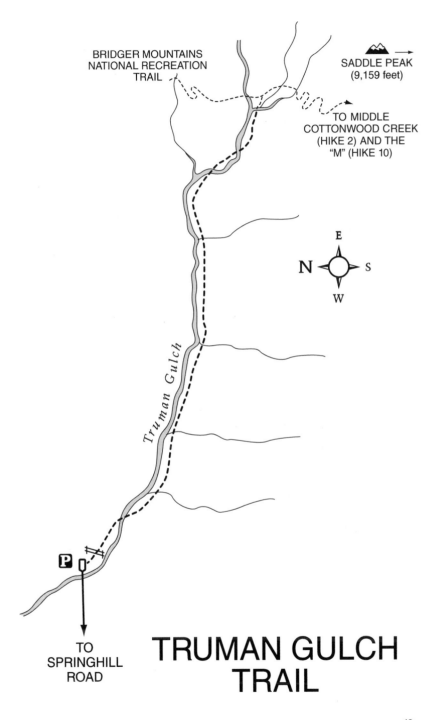

BRIDGER MOUNTAINS
NATIONAL RECREATION
TRAIL

SADDLE PEAK
(9,159 feet)

TO MIDDLE
COTTONWOOD CREEK
(HIKE 2) AND THE
"M" (HIKE 10)

E

N ← → S

W

Truman Gulch

P

TO
SPRINGHILL
ROAD

TRUMAN GULCH
TRAIL

Hike 2
Middle Cottonwood Creek

Hiking distance: 2.8 miles round trip
Hiking time: 1.5 hours
Elevation gain: 450 feet
Maps: U.S.G.S. Miser Creek and Saddle Peak
U.S.F.S. Gallatin National Forest West Half or East Half

Summary of hike: Middle Cottonwood Creek is a scenic creek with cascades, small waterfalls and pools. As the canyon narrows, there are colorful rock formations amid lush vegetation. The trail includes several creek crossings.

Driving directions: From I-90 and the 7th Avenue overpass, drive 2 miles north on 7th Avenue, which becomes West Frontage Road, to Springhill Road. Turn right (north) and continue 3.4 miles to Toohey Road on the right. There is a sign for Middle Cottonwood Creek. Turn right and drive 1.7 miles to Walker Road. Turn right again and continue 3.2 miles to the trailhead parking area at road's end.

Hiking directions: From the parking area, the trail heads east past three boulders and across a footbridge over the creek. Continue up the canyon 0.4 miles to a log creek crossing. Once across, the trail stays close to the cascades and pools of the creek. At 0.8 miles, the canyon narrows and there are dynamic moss-covered rock formations. Boulder hop across the creek as the trail crosses over to the north side of the creek. At one mile the trail joins with the Bridger Mountains National Recreation Trail. (This trail crosses over the creek to the right and continues 6 miles uphill to the "M," Hike 10.) Continue straight ahead up the canyon. The trail switchbacks up the mountain away from the creek. At 1.4 miles is a ridge overlooking the surrounding drainages. This is our turnaround spot. To return, retrace your steps.

To hike further, the trail eventually leads to Truman Gulch (Hike 1), two drainages north, and Fairy Lake (Hike 5).

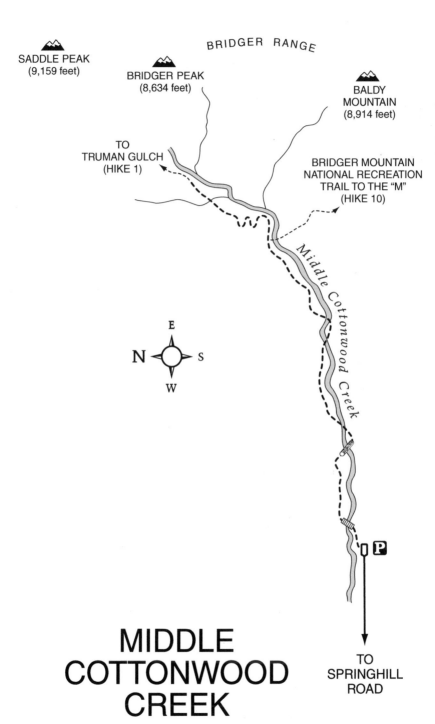

BRIDGER RANGE

SADDLE PEAK
(9,159 feet)

BRIDGER PEAK
(8,634 feet)

BALDY
MOUNTAIN
(8,914 feet)

TO
TRUMAN GULCH
(HIKE 1)

BRIDGER MOUNTAIN
NATIONAL RECREATION
TRAIL TO THE "M"
(HIKE 10)

Middle Cottonwood Creek

E
N ◇ S
W

TO
SPRINGHILL
ROAD

MIDDLE COTTONWOOD CREEK

Hike 3
Sypes Canyon Trail

Hiking distance: 4 miles round trip
Hiking time: 2 hours
Elevation gain: 1,000 feet
Maps: U.S.G.S. Bozeman and Kelly Creek
U.S.F.S. Gallatin National Forest West Half or East Half

Summary of hike: Sypes Canyon follows a creek-fed canyon on the west side of the Bridger Mountains. The hike leads through a lush, shady forest and up the south canyon wall. The hike ends at an overlook with outstanding views of the Gallatin Valley, Bozeman and the Madison and Tobacco Root Mountain Ranges.

Driving directions: From I-90 and the 7th Avenue overpass, drive 2 miles north on 7th Avenue, which becomes West Frontage Road, to Springhill Road. Turn right and drive 1.5 miles to Sypes Canyon Road. Turn right and continue 3.2 miles to Churn Road. Turn right and go 50 yards to the signed trailhead at the end of the road.

Hiking directions: Head east past the trail sign and through a grassy, fenced access. Enter a lush forest canopy into Sypes Canyon on the right side of Sypes Creek. Cross over to the north side of the creek, and head up the north wall of the canyon above Sypes Creek. At a half mile, the trail reaches a ridge. Descend alongside a rock wall cliff into the lush, forested canyon. Curve right at one mile, heading south up the canyon while skirting the edge of the national forest boundary. Begin an ascent through the shade of a lodgepole pine forest to a saddle by a trail sign with a view of the valley. Bear left 200 yards to a vista overlook of Bozeman and the Madison Range. This is a great spot to relax and enjoy the views before returning back down Sypes Canyon.

To hike further, the trail continues to climb to a junction with the Bridger Mountains National Recreation Trail.

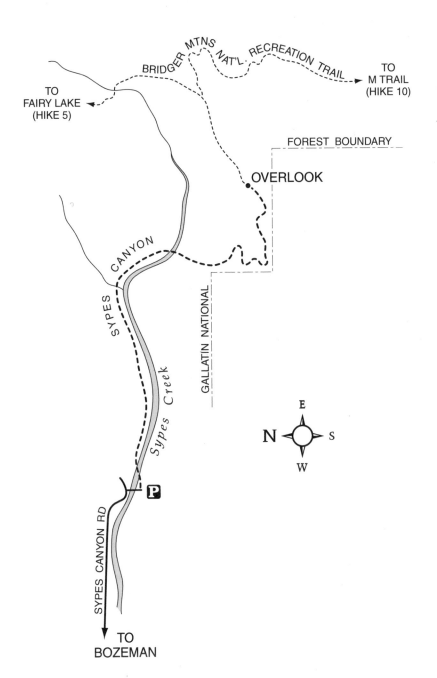

BRIDGER MTNS NAT'L. RECREATION TRAIL

TO M TRAIL
(HIKE 10)

TO FAIRY LAKE
(HIKE 5)

FOREST BOUNDARY

OVERLOOK

SYPES CANYON

GALLATIN NATIONAL

Sypes Creek

E
N ← ☼ → S
W

P

SYPES CANYON RD

TO BOZEMAN

SYPES CANYON TRAIL

Hike 4
Stone Creek Trail

Hiking distance: 4 miles round trip
Hiking time: 2 hours
Elevation gain: 400 feet
Maps: U.S.G.S. Saddle Peak and Grassy Mountain
U.S.F.S. Gallatin National Forest East Half or West Half

Summary of hike: The Stone Creek Trail winds through a beautiful rolling mountain and meadow landscape. It is more of a stroll through the mountains than a backcountry hike, as the trail is a vehicle restricted logging road. The road heads up the drainage along the north bank of cascading Stone Creek. This is also a popular cross-country ski trail.

Driving directions: From Main Street in downtown Bozeman, head north on North Rouse Avenue. The road curves right and becomes Bridger Canyon Drive (Highway 86). Stone Creek Road is on the right side of the road 12 miles from Main Street. Turn right and continue 1.2 miles to the Forest Service gate. Parking pullouts are located on both sides of the road.

Hiking directions: From the parking area, hike east up the forested canyon road past the Forest Service gate. At 0.5 miles, an old abandoned log house sits to the right of the trail by Stone Creek. At 1.2 miles, the Moody Creek Trail heads up Moody Gulch. Stay on the Stone Creek Road. At two miles, the road approaches the end of the draw. The road curves sharply to the right and crosses Stone Creek, continuing to the right. A posted foot trail leaves the road at this curve and crosses the creek to the left. From here, the trail ascends steeply out of the canyon. This is our turnaround spot. Take the same road back to the trailhead.

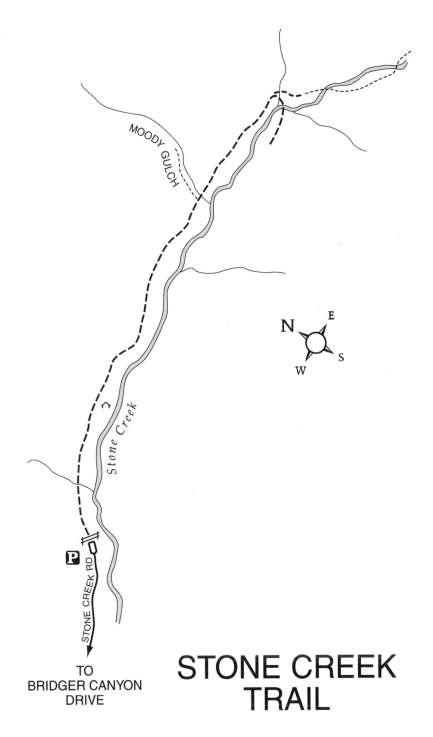

MOODY GULCH

N
E
W
S

Stone Creek

P

STONE CREEK RD

TO
BRIDGER CANYON
DRIVE

STONE CREEK
TRAIL

Hike 5
Fairy Lake Trail

Hiking distance: 1.2 mile loop
Hiking time: 40 minutes
Elevation gain: 100 feet
Maps: U.S.G.S. Sacagawea Peak
U.S.F.S. Gallatin National Forest East Half

Summary of hike: Fairy Lake is a picture-perfect, tree-lined lake sitting in a forested bowl at the base of Sacagawea Mountain. The lake receives heavy use due to its close proximity to the Fairy Lake Campground, located a short quarter mile from the lake. The trail loops around the perimeter of the lake. This high mountain area is a great place to have a picnic and spend the day.

Driving directions: From Main Street in downtown Bozeman, head north on North Rouse Avenue, and drive 21.4 miles to the signed Fairy Lake turnoff on the left. En route, the road curves right and becomes Bridger Canyon Drive (Highway 86). The turnoff is 0.9 miles past the Battle Ridge Campground. Turn left on Fairy Lake Road. Drive 6.1 miles on the unpaved road to the Fairy Lake Campground. Park at the signed trailhead on the left.

Hiking directions: Take the signed Fairy Lake Trail a quarter mile gently downhill to the north shore of the lake. At the shoreline bear left, following the forested route along the east shore of the lake. Rock hop across Fairy Creek, the outlet stream. A fisherman trail follows the shoreline, hugging the edge of the water. Various side paths meander through the forest and reconnect at the shoreline. Loop around to the west end of the lake. The path continues along the water's edge below the rocky cliffs of Sacagawea Mountain. After completing the loop, return to the left.

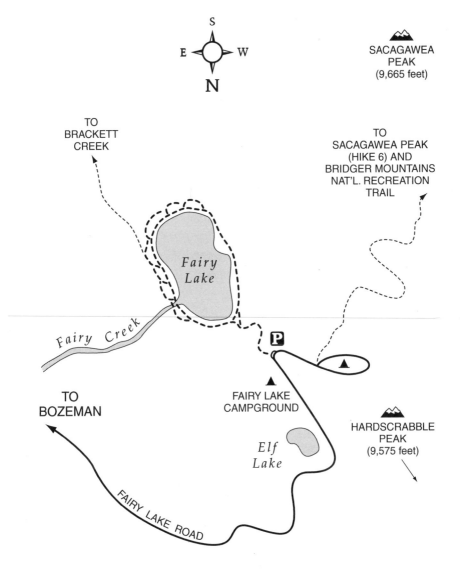

S
E ✦ W
N

SACAGAWEA
PEAK
(9,665 feet)

TO
BRACKETT
CREEK

TO
SACAGAWEA PEAK
(HIKE 6) AND
BRIDGER MOUNTAINS
NAT'L. RECREATION
TRAIL

Fairy Lake

Fairy Creek

P

TO
BOZEMAN

FAIRY LAKE
CAMPGROUND

HARDSCRABBLE
PEAK
(9,575 feet)

Elf Lake

FAIRY LAKE ROAD

FAIRY LAKE TRAIL

Hike 6
Sacagawea Peak

Hiking distance: 4 miles round trip
Hiking time: 3 hours
Elevation gain: 2,000 feet
Maps: U.S.G.S. Sacagawea Peak
U.S.F.S. Gallatin National Forest East Half

Summary of hike: Sacagawea Peak, at 9,665 feet, is the highest peak in the Bridger Range, part of the Gallatin National Forest. The trail climbs up Sacagawea Mountain to a saddle between Sacagawea Peak and Hardscrabble Peak at the Bridger Divide. From the divide the trail winds up to the rocky summit for fantastic views of mountain ranges in every direction. To the south are the Gallatin and Madison Ranges; the Big Belts lie to the north; the Elkhorns and Tobacco Roots lie to the west; and the Crazies are to the east.

Driving directions: From Main Street in downtown Bozeman, head north on North Rouse Avenue, and drive 21.4 miles to the signed Fairy Lake turnoff on the left. En route, the road curves right and becomes Bridger Canyon Drive (Highway 86). The turnoff is 0.9 miles past the Battle Ridge Campground. Turn left on Fairy Lake Road. Drive 6.1 miles on the unpaved road to the Fairy Lake Campground. Turn right and park 0.1 mile ahead at the signed trail on the left.

Hiking directions: From the signed trail, take the right fork through the conifer forest. Traverse the hillside up several switchbacks while great views open up to the east. Cross the northern edge of a meadow abundant with wildflowers. Switchbacks lead up the exposed rocky bowl at the head of the drainage. Climb up to the ridge on the Bridger Divide at 8,963 feet. At the divide are cairns and a signed junction. The right fork leads up to Hardscrabble Peak (Hike 7). Take the left fork and follow the ridge south. Pass a signed junction on the right, heading down the mountain to Corby Creek and North

Cottonwood Creek. Continue gaining elevation southeast along the ridge. Bear left at a junction with the Bridger Mountains National Recreation Trail, and head north for the final ascent to the peak. After enjoying the incredible views at the summit, return along the same path.

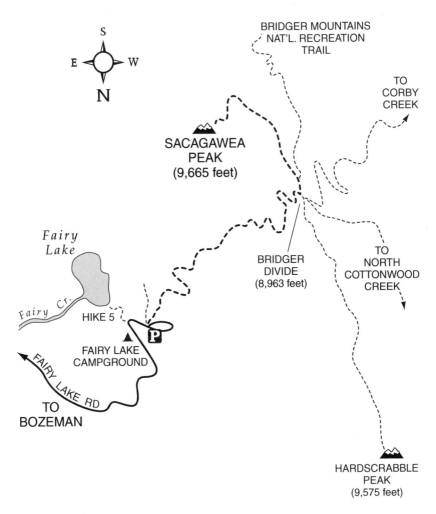

SACAGAWEA PEAK

Hike 7
Hardscrabble Peak

Hiking distance: 4 miles round trip
Hiking time: 3 hours
Elevation gain: 1,900 feet
Maps: U.S.G.S. Sacagawea Peak
       U.S.F.S. Gallatin National Forest East Half

Summary of hike: Hardscrabble Peak sits to the north of Sacagawea Peak in the Bridger Mountains. The mountain has three peaks. This hike leads to the southernmost peak at 9,575 feet. The trail follows the drainage between Sacagawea and Hardscrabble Peaks to the 8,963-foot saddle on the Bridger Divide. From Hardscrabble Peak are views of six surrounding mountain ranges—the Gallatin, Madison, Crazies, Tobacco Roots, Elkhorns and Big Belts.

Driving directions: From Main Street in downtown Bozeman, head north on North Rouse Avenue, and drive 21.4 miles to the signed Fairy Lake turnoff on the left. En route, the road curves right and becomes Bridger Canyon Drive (Highway 86). The turnoff is 0.9 miles past the Battle Ridge Campground. Turn left on Fairy Lake Road. Drive 6.1 miles on the unpaved road to the Fairy Lake Campground. Turn right and park 0.1 mile ahead at the signed trail on the left.

Hiking directions: Head south at the signed trail on the right fork through the shady forest. A series of switchbacks lead up the mountain, offering views to the east. Cross a grassy, wildflower-covered meadow, and begin the exposed climb up the rocky bowl. Switchbacks lead up to the 8,963-foot ridge at the Bridger Divide and a signed junction. The left fork (Hike 6) leads to Sacagawea Peak, the highest peak in the Bridger Mountains. Take the right fork and follow the ridge north, gaining 675 feet from the saddle to the peak. After marveling at the vistas from the rocky peak, return along the same path.

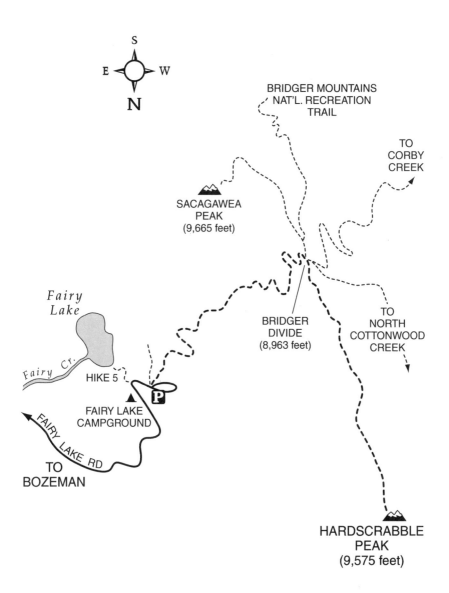

S

E ⊕ W

N

BRIDGER MOUNTAINS
NAT'L. RECREATION
TRAIL

TO
CORBY
CREEK

SACAGAWEA
PEAK
(9,665 feet)

Fairy Lake

Fairy Cr.

BRIDGER
DIVIDE
(8,963 feet)

TO
NORTH
COTTONWOOD
CREEK

HIKE 5

P

FAIRY LAKE
CAMPGROUND

FAIRY LAKE RD

TO
BOZEMAN

HARDSCRABBLE
PEAK
(9,575 feet)

HARDSCRABBLE PEAK

Hike 8
East Gallatin River Trail and Glen Lake
East Gallatin Recreation Area
(Bozeman Beach)

Hiking distance: 1.2 miles round trip
Hiking time: 30 minutes
Elevation gain: Level
Maps: U.S.G.S. Bozeman

Summary of hike: The East Gallatin River Trail begins at Bozeman Beach and Glen Lake, a man-made lake with a 300-foot beachfront in the East Gallatin Recreation Area. The recreation area has picnic shelters and a fishing dock. The trail leaves the lake and crosses a field, an old abandoned landfill, along the serpentine East Gallatin River. There are various fishing accesses along the route.

Driving directions: From Main Street in downtown Bozeman, head north on North Rouse Avenue 1.4 miles to Griffin Drive. Turn left and drive 0.3 miles to Manley Road. Turn right and continue 0.6 miles to the signed East Gallatin Recreation Area. Turn right and drive a short distance to the parking lot on the east side of Glen Lake.

Hiking directions: Cross the park lawn away from Glen Lake, heading east to the signed trail. Walk through the lush foliage into the grassy meadow. The path loops through the meadow to a trail split. Take the left fork towards the East Gallatin River. The trail heads upstream parallel to the winding contours of the river. Several narrow side paths lead down to the banks of the river. The trail currently ends 0.6 miles ahead at the edge of the river near a scenic mobile home compound. The Gallatin Valley Land Trust has future plans to connect the trail with the Story Mill Spur Trail (Hike 9) via a bridge crossing the river. The trail will include two loop paths along the east side of the river. Return along the same trail back to Glen Lake, or loop back through the meadow on the old unpaved road.

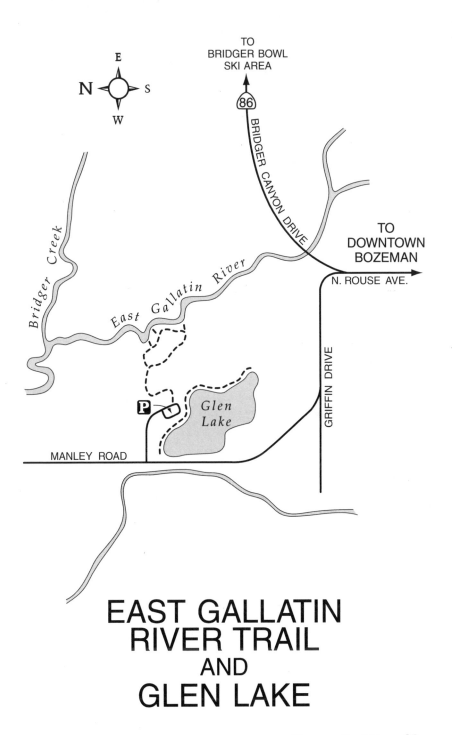

EAST GALLATIN
RIVER TRAIL
AND
GLEN LAKE

Hike 9
Story Mill Spur Trail

Hiking distance: 2 miles round trip
Hiking time: 1 hour
Elevation gain: Level
Maps: U.S.G.S. Bozeman

Summary of hike: Back in 1883, Story Mill was the largest flour mill in Montana. It was also the first business in Bozeman serviced by the railroad. Railroad tracks, known as the Story Mill Spur, lead 4,400 feet to the historic mill. The Story Mill Spur Trail is an interpretive trail along the railroad right-of-way. After nine years of dedicated work by the Gallatin Valley Land Trust, this historic trail has become a reality. The trail crosses Rocky Creek, where benches have been placed in the shade of the cottonwood trees. The hike passes the Bozeman Livestock stockyards and the historic Story Mill to Bridger Canyon Drive.

Driving directions: From Main Street in downtown Bozeman, take North Wallace Street 0.6 miles to East Tamarack Street. Turn right and park alongside the road. The trail is on the north side of the railroad tracks.

Hiking directions: Walk north on North Wallace Street 0.1 mile, crossing the railroad tracks to the signed trail on the left side of the road. Take the trail along the right side of the railroad tracks heading north. Cross over the tracks and under I-90. The trail narrows and the shrub-lined path heads directly towards the Bridger Mountains. Continue past farmhouses, barns and horses. Cross a wooden footbridge over Rocky Creek, and pass the cottonwood grove by the historic remains of the Gallatin Valley Auction Yard. The trail connects with the unpaved Story Mill Road. Bear left past the mills to the signed footpath on the left side of the road. The trail currently ends at Bridger Drive. Future plans are in progress to connect this trail with East Gallatin Park (Hike 8) and the M Trail (Hike 10). To return, take the same route back.

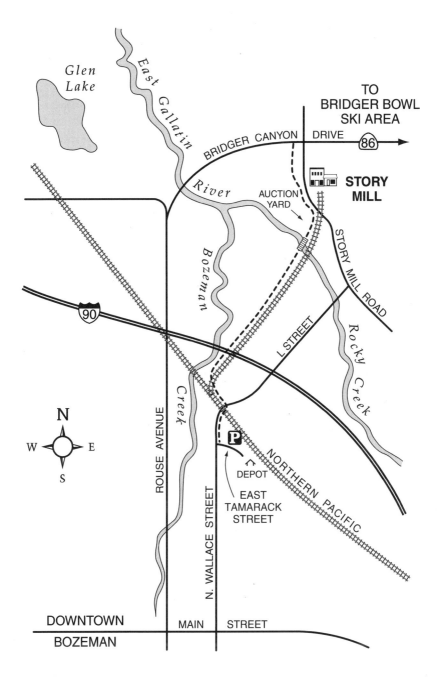

STORY MILL SPUR TRAIL

Hike 10
M Trail

Hiking distance: 1.6 mile loop
Hiking time: 1 hour
Elevation gain: 850 feet
Maps: U.S.G.S. Kelly Creek
U.S.F.S. Gallatin National Forest East Half

Summary of hike: The Montana State University "M" is located at the mouth of Bridger Canyon on the south flanks of Baldy Mountain. The "M" was created by MSU students in 1915. The 250-foot whitewashed rock "M" has two access routes. The right fork follows the ridge for a short and steep hike. The left fork switchbacks through a fir and juniper forest, making a more gradual ascent. The left fork is the beginning of the Bridger Mountains National Recreation Trail, a 21-mile ridge route following the contours of the Bridger Range to Fairy Lake (Hike 5). This hike to the "M" climbs up the steeper ridge route and descends through the forest via the switchbacks.

Driving directions: From Main Street in downtown Bozeman, head north on North Rouse Avenue 4.2 miles to the signed trailhead on the left. En route, the road curves right and becomes Bridger Canyon Drive (Highway 86). Turn left into the trailhead parking lot.

Hiking directions: Head north past the trailhead gate and picnic area to a junction with wide, clearly defined trails. Begin the loop by taking the right fork in a counter-clockwise direction. Head steeply up the ridge, mercilessly up to the base of the "M." Beyond the "M" is a junction. The right fork loops back to the top of the "M" and the ridge. The left fork levels out and begins the return loop. Bear left at a second junction and begin the descent on the switchbacks to a junction with the Bridger Mountains National Recreation Trail (Trail #534). Go left, returning to the base of the mountain, and complete the loop. Return to the trailhead on the right.

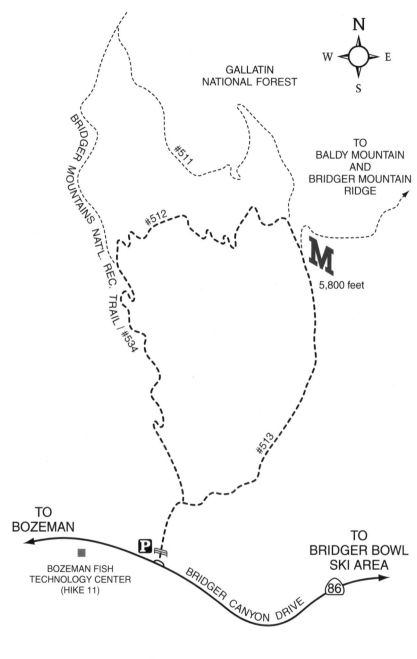

N
W E
S

GALLATIN
NATIONAL FOREST

BRIDGER MOUNTAINS NATL. REC. TRAIL / #534

#511

#512

TO
BALDY MOUNTAIN
AND
BRIDGER MOUNTAIN
RIDGE

M

5,800 feet

#513

TO
BOZEMAN

BOZEMAN FISH
TECHNOLOGY CENTER
(HIKE 11)

P

BRIDGER CANYON DRIVE

86

TO
BRIDGER BOWL
SKI AREA

M TRAIL

Hike 11
Bozeman Fish Technology Center
Nature Trail

Open 8:00 a.m. to 4:00 p.m. daily

Hiking distance: 0.5 mile loop
Hiking time: 30 minutes
Elevation gain: 50 feet
Maps: U.S.G.S. Kelly Creek
Bozeman Fish Technology Center tour map

Summary of hike: The Bozeman Fish Technology Center is a hatchery and research area with a charming nature loop along Bridger Creek. The hatchery includes fish runs with observation walkways, a pond and picnic area.

Driving directions: From Main Street in downtown Bozeman, head north on North Rouse Avenue 4.1 miles to the signed Bozeman Fish Technology Center on the right, across the road from the M Trail (Hike 10). En route, the road curves right and becomes Bridger Canyon Drive (Highway 86). Turn right and park in the visitor parking lot on the right.

Hiking directions: Take the log-lined path west past the metal sculptures of cutthroat trout and graylings. Head up the hillside through the grove of aspens and wild roses to an overlook of the Montana State University "M" (Hike 10) at a trail split. The right fork leads 20 yards and ends on a knoll. Bear left along the rolling hills, and descend to a wooden footbridge crossing a streambed. Go to the left and parallel Bridger Creek, heading upstream to the hatchery maintenance road. An arched bridge crosses the creek to the right to the housing area. Go to the left, following the road back to the parking lot. To the east of the parking lot are the fish raceways, a pond and picnic area.

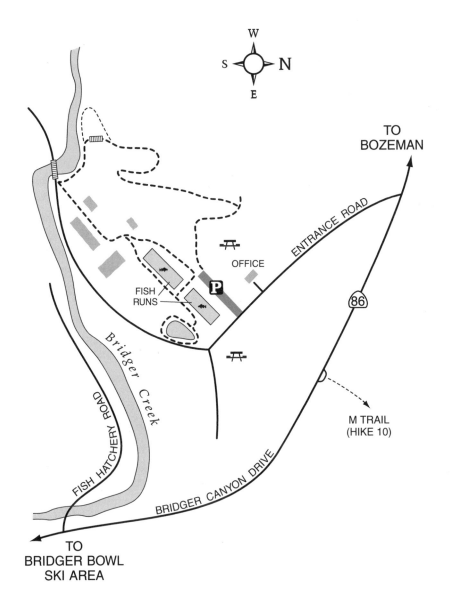

W N
S E

TO
BOZEMAN

ENTRANCE ROAD

OFFICE

86

FISH
RUNS

Bridger Creek

P

M TRAIL
(HIKE 10)

FISH HATCHERY ROAD

BRIDGER CANYON DRIVE

TO
BRIDGER BOWL
SKI AREA

BOZEMAN
FISH TECHNOLOGY
CENTER

Hike 12
Gallagator Trail

Hiking distance: 2.2 miles round trip
Hiking time: 1 hour
Elevation gain: Level
Maps: U.S.G.S. Bozeman

Summary of hike: The Gallagator Trail follows the route of the Gallagator Railroad Line, which took passengers between Bozeman and the Gallatin Gateway and abandoned in the late 1930s. The path begins at Burke Park at the base of Peets' Hill and crosses several bridges over Sourdough Creek and Mathew Bird Creek. The trail ends at a picnic area by the Museum of the Rockies. There are several street crossings along the route.

Driving directions: From Main Street at the east end of downtown Bozeman, drive south on South Church Avenue 0.4 miles to the parking area on the left, at the base of Peets' Hill across from Story Street.

Hiking directions: Cross South Church Avenue to the corner of Story Street. Take the signed trail southwest along the Gallagator Linear Park. Follow the wide, tree-lined path along an old railroad right-of-way. Cross a bridge over Sourdough Creek. At 0.2 miles, cross a second bridge over Mathew Bird Creek. Follow the creek past scenic neighborhood backyards. A side path meanders to the right and rejoins the main trail. Cross another bridge over Mathew Bird Creek, reaching Garfield Street at 0.5 miles. After crossing the road, follow the trail along the right side of the creek to a signed trail split with the Langhor Spur Trail, leading to Langhor Park on the left. Stay to the right, passing a pond on the left to South Willson Avenue. Cross the road and bear left 70 yards to Lincoln Street. Pick up the path again by the wooden trail posts on the southwest corner. Follow the hedge-lined path and to Kagy Boulevard. Cross the road to the Museum of the Rockies. Follow the path to a picnic area by the metal horse sculpture. To return, retrace your steps.

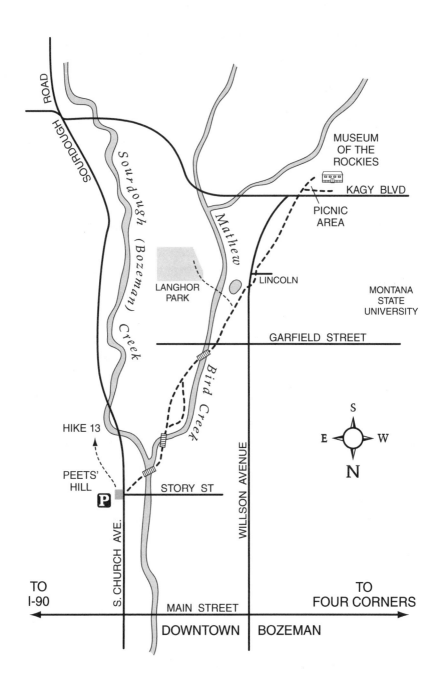

GALLAGATOR TRAIL

Hike 13
Chris Boyd—Highland Ridge Trail

Hiking distance: 4.4 miles round trip
Hiking time: 2 hours
Elevation gain: 100 feet
Maps: U.S.G.S. Bozeman

Summary of hike: The Highland Ridge Trail begins at Peets' Hill in Burke Park. From the top of the hill are great views of Bozeman and the Bridger, Madison and Gallatin Ranges. The beginning of the trail along the ridge in Burke Park has been renamed and dedicated to Chris Boyd, founder of the Gallatin Valley Land Trust. Benches are placed along the ridge. The trail skirts the edge of a subdivision and heads south through rolling grasslands, connecting with the Painted Hills Trail (Hike 14).

Driving directions: From Main Street at the east end of downtown Bozeman, drive south on South Church Avenue 0.4 miles to the parking area on the left, at the base of Peets' Hill across from Story Street.

Hiking directions: Take the main trail south up to the top of Peets' Hill. From the top are several paths. The Chris Boyd Trail, which begins in Lindley Park, heads south and follows the hillside ridge through Burke Park. Pass the Wortman Spur Trail on the right that leads down the hillside to Church Avenue. Continue along the ridge 0.7 miles to a signed junction with the Simkins Spur Trail at the water tower. Bear left on the Highland Ridge Trail. Follow the wooden rail fence to the east, between farmland to the north and a row of homes to the south, to Highland Boulevard. Go to the left 75 yards on the paved bike path, and cross the road, picking up the signed trail again. The path curves around the perimeter of New Hyalite View subdivision and curves south through the rolling grasslands. At 2.3 miles, the trail forks. Curve left, reaching Kagy Boulevard. Follow the Kagy Connector Trail east, crossing the road to the Painted Hills Trailhead 0.4 miles ahead. Return on the same path.

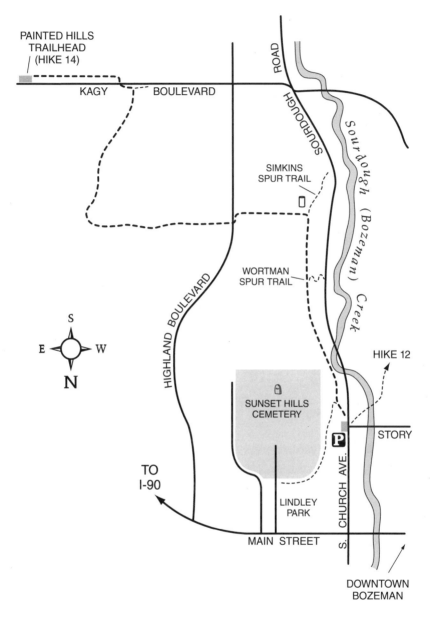

CHRIS BOYD–
HIGHLAND RIDGE TRAIL

Hike 14
Painted Hills Trail

Hiking distance: 2.5 miles round trip
Hiking time: 1 hour
Elevation gain: Level
Maps: U.S.G.S. Bozeman

Summary of hike: The Painted Hills Trail begins near the south end of the Highland Ridge Trail (Hike 13). The Kagy Connector Trail links these two trails together. The Painted Hills Trail passes through a dedicated parkland along a gully near the Painted Hills subdivision. The path heads south, crossing a small meandering stream. The trail currently ends at a private property fenceline. The Gallatin Valley Land Trust is working towards extending the trail to connect with the Triple Tree Trail (Hike 16).

Driving directions: From Main Street at the east end of downtown Bozeman, drive south on South Church Avenue 1.6 miles to Kagy Boulevard. (South Church Avenue becomes Sourdough Road after Kagy Boulevard.) Turn left on Kagy Boulevard, and drive 0.9 miles to the trailhead parking area on the right.

Hiking directions: Head south past the trail sign, following the east edge of the draw. Continue across a series of small rises and dips. Cross a wooden footbridge over a seasonal drainage. At 0.6 miles, cross a paved subdivision road. Pick up the trail again and cross another wooden footbridge. Bear left on the narrow footpath and continue up the draw. The trail currently ends at 1.25 miles at a private property fenceline. Return by retracing your steps.

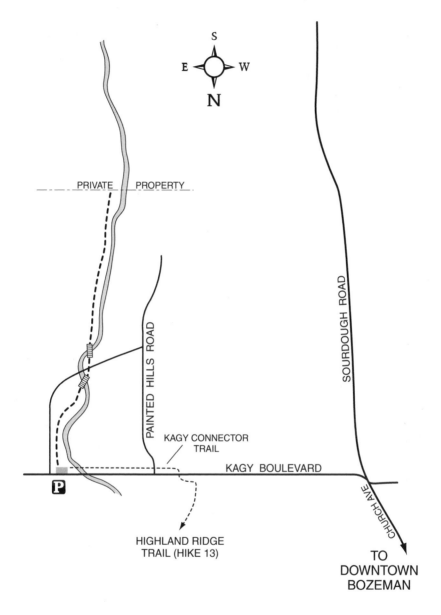

S
E W
N

PRIVATE PROPERTY

SOURDOUGH ROAD

PAINTED HILLS ROAD

KAGY CONNECTOR
TRAIL

KAGY BOULEVARD

CHURCH AVE

P

HIGHLAND RIDGE
TRAIL (HIKE 13)

TO
DOWNTOWN
BOZEMAN

PAINTED HILLS
TRAIL

Hike 15
Sourdough Trail

Hiking distance: 3.2 miles round trip
Hiking time: 1.5 hours
Elevation gain: 100 feet
Maps: U.S.G.S. Bozeman

Summary of hike: The Sourdough Trail parallels Sourdough Creek under the shade of aspen and cottonwoods. After crossing over the creek, the path breaks out into the grassy meadows and skirts the Valley View Golf Course. In the winter, the Sourdough Trail is a popular cross-country ski trail.

Driving directions: From Main Street at the east end of downtown Bozeman, drive south on South Church Avenue 3.2 miles to Goldenstein Lane. (South Church Avenue becomes Sourdough Road.) Turn right and drive 0.5 miles to the signed trail on the right, just after crossing the bridge over Sourdough Creek. Park in the small pullouts along either side of the road.

Hiking directions: Head north on the beautiful forested path along the west side of Sourdough Creek. Short side paths on the right lead to the creek. The trail winds through the shady forest, hugging the banks of the creek. At 0.3 miles, cross a footbridge over Sourdough Creek, reaching a trail split at a half mile. The left fork is the main trail. For a great side trip, detour to the right, and bear right at a second trail split to a 60-foot wooden bridge over the creek to Gardner park. Return to the main trail, and cross the creek to a signed junction with the Sundance Trail on the left. Stay on the Sourdough Trail, crossing another bridge over Nash-Spring Creek. Continue along the left side of the creek between pastures and the golf course. The path exits on Graf Street just south of Spring Meadow Drive. Go to the right, picking up the signed footpath 100 yards ahead on the right. Cross the open meadow lined with aspens on the east side of Mathew Bird Creek. Continue north between the homes to the trail's end on Fairway Drive.

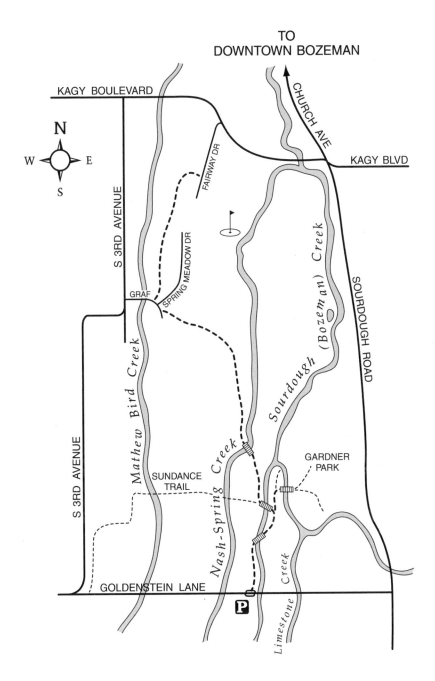

TO
DOWNTOWN BOZEMAN

KAGY BOULEVARD

CHURCH AVE

KAGY BLVD

N
W   E
S

S 3RD AVENUE

FAIRWAY DR

SPRING MEADOW DR

GRAF

Sourdough (Bozeman) Creek

SOURDOUGH ROAD

Mathew Bird Creek

Nash-Spring Creek

SUNDANCE
TRAIL

GARDNER
PARK

S 3RD AVENUE

GOLDENSTEIN LANE

P

Limestone Creek

SOURDOUGH TRAIL

Hike 16
Triple Tree Trail

Hiking distance: 4.5 miles round trip
Hiking time: 2 hours
Elevation gain: 800 feet
Maps: U.S.G.S. Wheeler Mountain and Mount Ellis

Summary of hike: The Triple Tree Trail begins on a grassy ridge, crosses Limestone Creek and winds through a shady woodland. The trail loops through the forest on Montana state land to a hilltop knoll in a wildflower-covered meadow. From the summit are 360-degree views of the Bozeman valley and the Gallatin, Madison, Tobacco Root and Bridger Ranges.

Driving directions: From Main Street in downtown Bozeman, drive south on South Church Avenue 4.6 miles to the signed parking lot on the left. The parking lot is 200 feet south of Triple Tree Road. (South Church Avenue becomes Sourdough Road after Kagy Boulevard.)

Hiking directions: Follow the wide grassy path east past the trailhead sign, and cross the rolling slopes. Enter an aspen grove and cross two footbridges over Limestone Creek. Emerge from the forest into the open meadow, and climb the slope to a signed junction at one mile. The left fork continues across the grasslands and crosses several subdivision roads. Take the right fork and follow the buck fence down into the drainage. Cross the bridge over Limestone Creek and another bridge over the wetlands. Ascend the hill into the forest to a trail split at 1.5 miles. Take the right fork, beginning the loop, and head up the west side of the draw into state land. Bear sharply to the right, and climb up the hillside. Follow the ridge up a winding course. At the top is a meadow with fantastic vistas. After enjoying the views, cross the meadow and begin the descent into the forested drainage. Head down the draw along the right side of a trickling stream. Near the bottom, cross the stream, completing the loop. Retrace your steps to return.

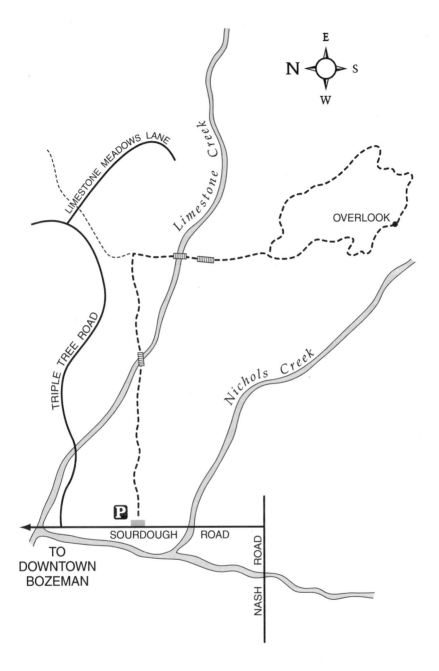

TRIPLE TREE TRAIL

Hike 17
Bozeman Creek Trail

Hiking distance: 0.5 to 22 miles round trip
Hiking time: 30 minutes and up
Elevation gain: Approximately 200 feet per mile
Maps: U.S.G.S. Wheeler Mountain and Mount Ellis
Crystal Bench Maps — Bozeman, Montana

Summary of hike: The Bozeman Creek Trail is located in Sourdough Canyon directly south of Bozeman. Its close proximity to Bozeman makes this a popular trail for hikers and bikers. The trail is an old logging road with a gradual ascent that follows the creek through a spruce and fir forest. The trail leads eleven miles up canyon to Mystic Lake.

Driving directions: From the east end of downtown Bozeman, drive south on South Church Avenue 5.2 miles to Nash Road. (South Church Avenue becomes Sourdough Road after Kagy Boulevard.) Turn right on Nash Road, and continue 0.2 miles to Sourdough Canyon Road on the left. Turn left and drive 0.9 miles to the trailhead parking area at road's end.

Hiking directions: From the parking area, pass the trailhead gate and head southeast along the wide trail. The trail follows Sourdough Canyon uphill parallel to Bozeman Creek. It climbs gradually but steadily. The trail continues alongside the northeast side of Bozeman Creek to Mystic Lake, 11 miles from the trailhead. Choose your own hiking distance, and return along the same trail.

To hike or bike further, at Mystic Lake the trail connects with the Bear Canyon drainage, Hyalite Reservoir and several other trails.

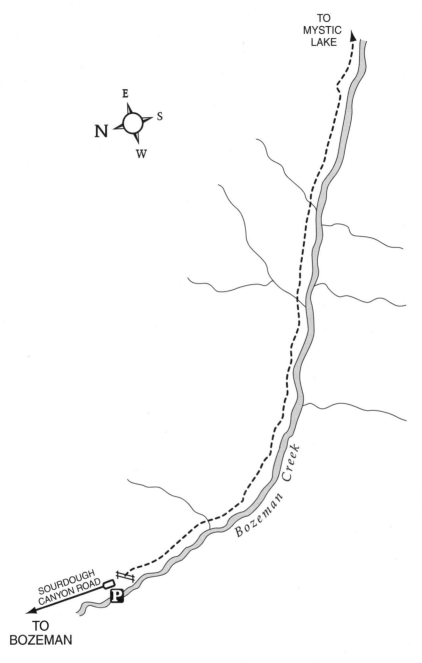

TO
MYSTIC
LAKE

E

N ⊙ S

W

Bozeman Creek

SOURDOUGH
CANYON ROAD

P

TO
BOZEMAN

BOZEMAN CREEK TRAIL

Hike 18
Leverich Canyon Trail

Hiking distance: 3.4 miles round trip
Hiking time: 2 hours
Elevation gain: 1,100 feet
Maps: U.S.G.S. Wheeler Mountain

Summary of hike: Leverich Canyon is a beautiful, narrow canyon south of Bozeman between Sourdough Canyon and Hyalite Canyon. The trail follows Leverich Creek for the first half of the hike. It passes an old miner's cabin and climbs to the top of the canyon. From the top are great views of Bozeman, Sourdough Canyon and the Bridger Mountains.

Driving directions: From Main Street at the west end of Bozeman, drive south on 19th Avenue for 5 miles to Nash Road. Turn left and drive 0.4 miles to South Third Road. Turn right and continue one mile to the end of the pavement. Follow the narrow unpaved lane straight ahead for one mile to the trailhead parking lot. At 0.8 miles, two road moguls make it difficult to drive. If so, park and walk 0.2 miles up the road.

Hiking directions: Take the footpath heading south from the south end of the parking area. The trail immediately crosses Leverich Creek three times. Follow the narrow canyon uphill along the watercourse. At 0.8 miles cross Leverich Creek to the left and head uphill, away from the creek. At 0.9 miles is a sharp right bend in the trail. On the right side of the bend is a mine and an old log cabin. The hike becomes steeper and corkscrews its way up the mountain. Near the top, the trail levels out and traverses the mountainside 1,400 feet above Bozeman Creek. The trail ends at a junction with the Moser Jumpoff Road, a gravel logging road. Return back down the canyon.

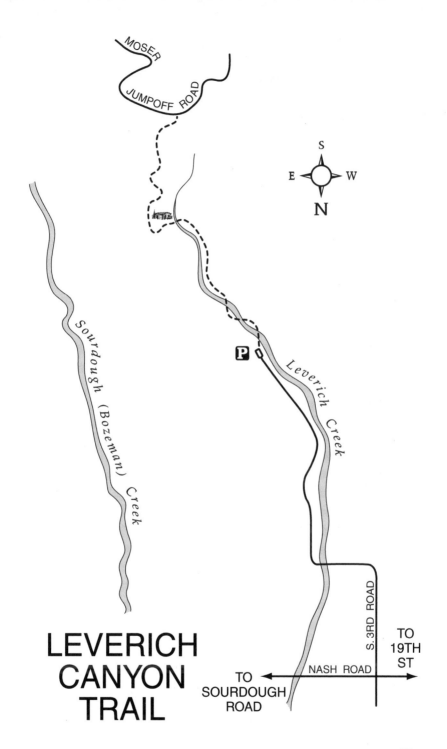

MOSER
JUMPOFF ROAD

S
E W
N

Sourdough (Bozeman) Creek

Leverich Creek

P

LEVERICH
CANYON
TRAIL

S. 3RD ROAD

TO
19TH
ST

TO
SOURDOUGH
ROAD

NASH ROAD

Hike 19
Kirk Hill (Loops 1 and 3)

Hiking distance: 1.7 miles round trip
Hiking time: 45 minutes
Elevation gain: 600 feet
Maps: U.S.G.S. Wheeler Mountain
Kirk Hill Nature Trail Map

Summary of hike: Kirk Hill has three loop trails. All three loops are self-guided interpretive trails. This hike follows a figure-8 pattern around Loops 1 and 3. At the top of Kirk Hill is an overlook with a panoramic map of the Madison Range identifying the peaks and canyons within sight. The trails are managed by the Museum of the Rockies and maintained by Kiwanis of the Bridgers.

Driving directions: From Main Street at the west end of Bozeman, drive south on 19th Avenue for 6.1 miles to the signed trailhead parking area on the left at a sharp right bend in the road. Turn left and park.

Hiking directions: Head south past the trailhead gate, and cross the grassy meadow. Head up the foothills through the shady forest, crossing the footbridge over the irrigation ditch. Switchbacks lead uphill to a signed junction at 0.5 miles. The left fork leads to Loop 2 (Hike 20). Take the right fork uphill to junction F. Bear left on the cut-across trail, and traverse the hillside on the near-level path to junction D. Head uphill to the right through the pine and fir forest, reaching junction E at the top of the hill. Go to the right, following the hilltop ridge past Rocky Mountain juniper. On the left is a short side path to a panoramic overlook of the Madison Range. Back on the main trail, begin the descent back to the cut-across trail at junction F. Bear right and traverse the hillside again to junction D. This time, bear left and descend through the forest to junction C. Bear left again, completing the figure-8 at junction B. Take the right fork downhill, returning to the trailhead.

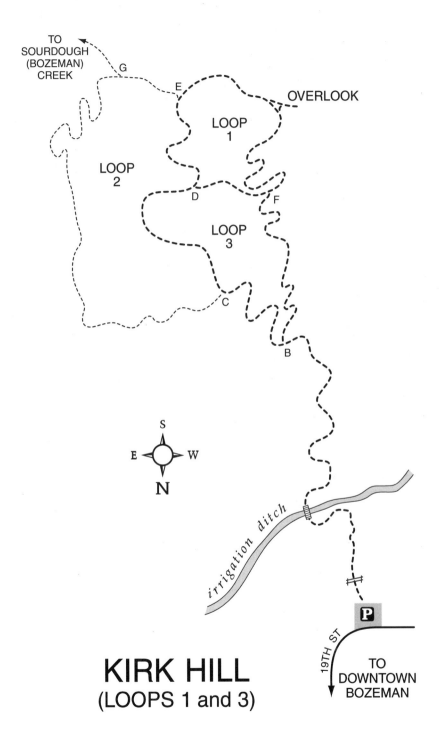

TO
SOURDOUGH
(BOZEMAN)
CREEK

G

E

OVERLOOK

LOOP
1

LOOP
2

D

F

LOOP
3

C

B

S

E ← ⊕ → W

N

irrigation ditch

P

19TH ST

TO
DOWNTOWN
BOZEMAN

KIRK HILL
(LOOPS 1 and 3)

Hike 20
Kirk Hill (Loop 2)

Hiking distance: 1.9 miles round trip
Hiking time: 1 hour
Elevation gain: 750 feet
Maps: U.S.G.S. Wheeler Mountain
Kirk Hill Nature Trail Map

Summary of hike: The Kirk Hill trails are interpretive loop trails highlighting information about the surrounding plant life. Kirk Hill sits above Leverich Canyon and Hodgman Canyon and borders the Gallatin National Forest. From the top, a trail connects Kirk Hill to Bozeman Creek and the Hyalite Creek divide. The Loop 2 Trail is the largest and steepest of the three loop trails.

Driving directions: From Main Street at the west end of Bozeman, drive south on 19th Avenue for 6.1 miles to the signed trailhead parking area on the left at a sharp right bend in the road. Turn left and park.

Hiking directions: Hike past the trailhead gate and cross the meadow, heading south. Enter the forest canopy up the sloping foothills. Cross the wooden footbridge over the irrigation ditch, and zigzag up the trail, steadily gaining elevation. At 0.5 miles is a signed junction. Take the left fork, weaving up the trail to junction C. Bear left, beginning the loop. Head east across the hillside through the forest of aspen, pine and fir. The path curves south and heads steadily uphill, including some short, steep ascents. Once at the top, the trail levels out and crosses the hilltop. Stay to the right past junction G, which leads to Bozeman Creek, to a junction with Loop 1. Go to the right, returning downhill to the cut-across trail dividing Loops 1 and 3. Again stay to the right, completing the loop at junction C. Go left, back to junction B. Take the right fork downhill, returning to the trailhead.

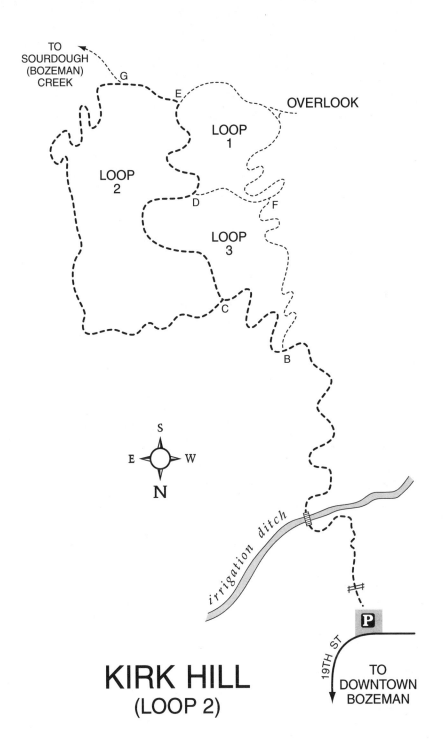

TO SOURDOUGH (BOZEMAN) CREEK

G

E

OVERLOOK

LOOP 1

LOOP 2

D

F

LOOP 3

C

B

S

E ← ✦ → W

N

irrigation ditch

P

19TH ST

TO DOWNTOWN BOZEMAN

KIRK HILL
(LOOP 2)

Hike 21
South Cottonwood Creek Trail

Hiking distance: 3.2 miles round trip
Hiking time: 2 hours
Elevation gain: 250 feet
Maps: U.S.G.S. Wheeler Mountain
      Crystal Bench Maps — Bozeman, Montana

Summary of hike: The South Cottonwood Creek Trail follows the creek upstream into beautiful Cottonwood Canyon through meadows and a forest. The South Cottonwood Creek Trail connects with the Langhor Trail at 2.4 miles and the History Rock Trail (Hike 23) at 6 miles.

Driving directions: From Bozeman, drive 4 miles west on Highway 191 (towards Four Corners) to Cottonwood Road on the left. Turn left and continue 7.6 miles to Cottonwood Canyon Road on the left. Turn left again and drive 2.1 miles to the trailhead parking area at road's end.

From Big Sky, drive 27.7 miles north on Highway 191 to Cottonwood Road on the right. Turn right and continue 4.8 miles to Cottonwood Canyon Road on the right. Turn right and drive 2.1 miles to the trailhead parking area at road's end.

Hiking directions: From the parking area, the well-marked trail switchbacks 150 feet up the hill before leveling off. The trail parallels Cottonwood Creek, slowly descending to the creek at 0.8 miles. Just before arriving at the creek, pass through a horse gate. Wade across the creek. (A footbridge is in the planning stages.) After crossing, climb a short hill to a meadow. From here, the trail hugs the hillside overlooking Cottonwood Creek. Again, the trail slowly descends to a second creek crossing. This is the turnaround spot.

For a longer hike, cross the creek and continue 0.8 miles to the next creek crossing and a junction with the Langhor Trail. The South Cottonwood Creek Trail continues several more miles south along the creek.

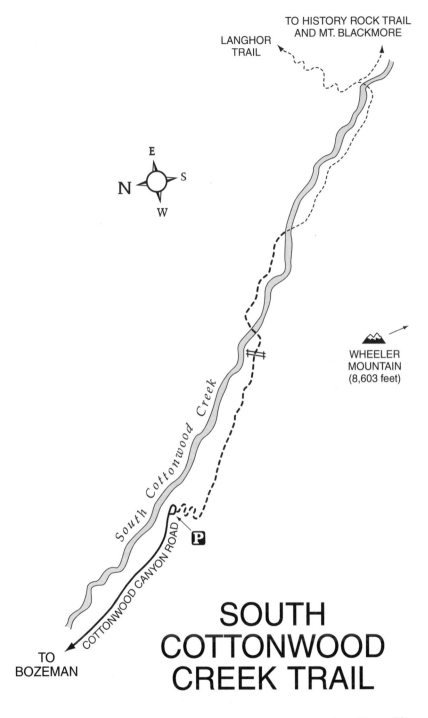

TO HISTORY ROCK TRAIL
AND MT. BLACKMORE

LANGHOR
TRAIL

N E S W

South Cottonwood Creek

WHEELER
MOUNTAIN
(8,603 feet)

COTTONWOOD CANYON ROAD

P

TO
BOZEMAN

SOUTH COTTONWOOD CREEK TRAIL

Hike 22
Langhor Loop Accessible Trail

Hiking distance: 0.3 mile loop to 2 miles round trip
Hiking time: 30 minutes to 1 hour
Elevation gain: Level
Maps: U.S.G.S. Wheeler Mountain
      U.S.F.S. Hyalite Drainage map
      Crystal Bench Maps — Bozeman, Montana

Summary of hike: The Langhor Loop Accessible Trail is a wheelchair accessible trail at the north end of the Langhor Campground on the banks of Hyalite Creek. The forested loop trail includes meadows with a gorgeous display of wildflowers, rock formations, several fishing accesses and sitting benches.

Driving directions: From Main Street and 19th Avenue in Bozeman, drive south on 19th Avenue, which becomes South 19th Road, 7 miles to Hyalite Canyon Road on the left—turn left. Continue 5.9 miles to the signed turnoff at the Langhor Campground. Turn right and make an immediate right again to the signed trailhead parking area 0.1 mile ahead.

Hiking directions: Pass the trailhead sign and head across the wooden bridge over Hyalite Creek. A well-defined side path follows Hyalite Creek upstream and ends at a massive rock formation. A fork to the right climbs up the hillside and scrambles along the cliffs above the creek. Head back to the bridge, and take the paved path to the north, following Hyalite Creek through a conifer forest. A short distance ahead is a trail fork, the beginning of the loop. Take the right fork downstream, staying close to the creek. Along the way, two paved side paths lead to the creek on the right. At the far end of the paved loop, a footpath continues north, following the creek through the forest. On the return portion of the paved loop, the trail continues through the forest past meadows with log benches. Complete the loop and return to the bridge.

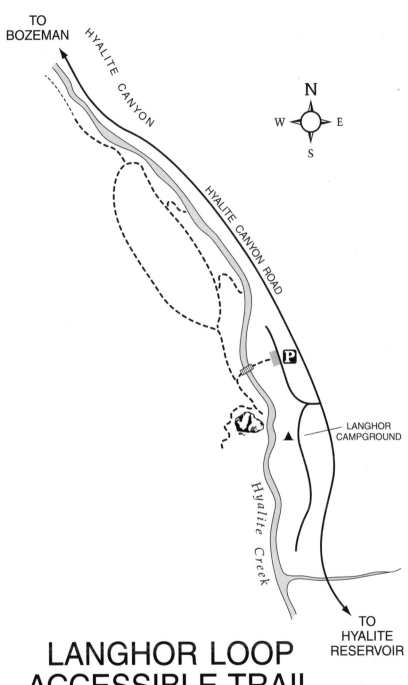

TO
BOZEMAN

HYALITE CANYON

HYALITE CANYON ROAD

N

W   E

S

P

LANGHOR
CAMPGROUND

Hyalite Creek

TO
HYALITE
RESERVOIR

LANGHOR LOOP
ACCESSIBLE TRAIL

Hike 23
History Rock Trail

Hiking distance: 2.4 miles round trip
Hiking time: 1 hour
Elevation gain: 300 feet
Maps: U.S.G.S. Fridley Peak
U.S.F.S. Hyalite Drainage Map
Crystal Bench Maps — Bozeman, Montana

Summary of hike: The trail to History Rock is a short uphill hike to an impressive rock formation with names dating back to the 1800s. Aside from the names with historical significance, you can also find "Juan loves Sylvia 1994."

Driving directions: From Main Street and 19th Avenue in Bozeman, drive south on 19th Avenue, which becomes South 19th Road, 7 miles to Hyalite Canyon Road on the left—turn left. Continue 8.8 miles to the History Rock turnoff on the right. Turn right and park 100 feet ahead in the trailhead parking area.

Hiking directions: From the parking area, the log-bordered trail heads southwest through a meadow. Past the meadow, the trail enters a forest and begins gaining elevation. At 1.2 miles the obvious and well-etched History Rock is on the right. This is the turnaround spot for the hike.

To hike further, the trail continues 1,000 feet up in two miles to Hyalite Divide before descending to South Cottonwood Creek drainage, four miles from History Rock. Return by taking the same path back.

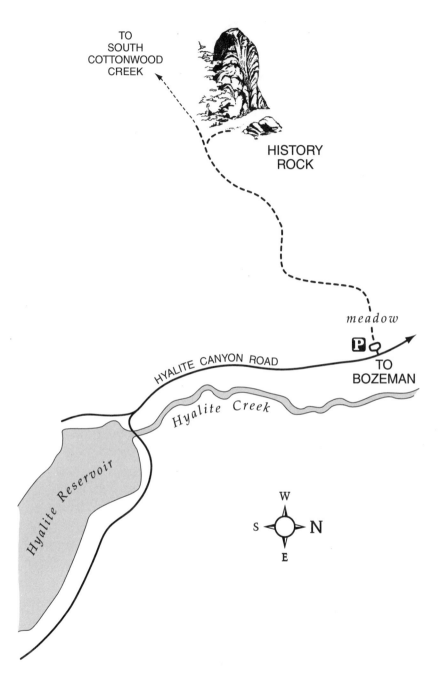

TO
SOUTH
COTTONWOOD
CREEK

HISTORY
ROCK

meadow

TO
BOZEMAN

HYALITE CANYON ROAD

Hyalite Creek

Hyalite Reservoir

W
S — N
E

HISTORY ROCK TRAIL

Hike 24
Blackmore Trail to Blackmore Lake

Hiking distance: 3.3 miles round trip
Hiking time: 2 hours
Elevation gain: 500 feet
Maps: U.S.G.S. Fridley Peak
      U.S.F.S. Hyalite Drainage Map
      Crystal Bench Maps — Bozeman, Montana

Summary of hike: The Blackmore Trail leads to Blackmore Lake at an altitude of 7,300 feet, then continues up to Mount Blackmore. The lake is surrounded by a dense pine forest, a meadow and the surrounding mountains of Mount Blackmore and Elephant Mountain. The trail begins at the west shore of Hyalite Reservoir.

Driving directions: From Main Street and 19th Avenue in Bozeman, drive south on 19th Avenue, which becomes South 19th Road, 7 miles to Hyalite Canyon Road on the left—turn left. Continue 9.9 miles to the trailhead parking area on the right. Hyalite Reservoir is to the left.

Hiking directions: From the parking area, take the signed Blackmore Trail to a log crossing over Blackmore Creek. Once over the creek, the path forks. The left branch leads to Crescent Lake—Hike 25. Stay on the Blackmore Trail bearing to the right. At 0.4 miles the trail crosses an old jeep road. The trail zigzags uphill through the forest, then levels out. As you near the lake, which is not within view, there is a short but steep descent that leads to the southeast corner of Blackmore Lake. The trail continues along the east side of the lake into a meadow where Blackmore Creek flows placidly. This is our turnaround spot. Return along the same trail.

To hike further, the trail continues 3 miles up to Mount Blackmore, then descends to South Cottonwood Creek.

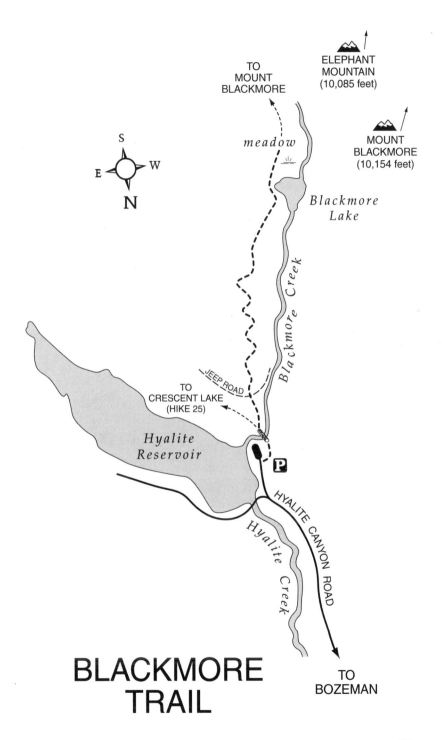

TO
MOUNT
BLACKMORE

ELEPHANT
MOUNTAIN
(10,085 feet)

meadow

MOUNT
BLACKMORE
(10,154 feet)

*Blackmore
Lake*

Blackmore Creek

JEEP ROAD

TO
CRESCENT LAKE
(HIKE 25)

S

W

E

N

*Hyalite
Reservoir*

P

HYALITE CANYON ROAD

Hyalite Creek

BLACKMORE
TRAIL

TO
BOZEMAN

Hike 25
Crescent Lake and
West Shore Loop

Hiking distance: 2.5 mile loop
Hiking time: 1.5 hours
Elevation gain: 240 feet
Maps: U.S.G.S. Fridley Peak
U.S.F.S. Hyalite Drainage Map
Crystal Bench Maps — Bozeman, Montana

Summary of hike: The trail to Crescent Lake is an easy meander through the forest to a small crescent-shaped lake. The return trail follows the shoreline of Hyalite Reservoir. This large recreational area is surrounded by picturesque mountains in every direction.

Driving directions: From Main Street and 19th Avenue in Bozeman, drive south on 19th Avenue, which becomes South 19th Road, 7 miles to Hyalite Canyon Road on the left—turn left. Continue 9.9 miles to the trailhead parking area on the right. Hyalite Reservoir is to the left.

Hiking directions: The hike begins on the Blackmore Trail at the north end of the parking area. A short distance from the trailhead is a log crossing over Blackmore Creek, an inlet stream of the Hyalite Reservoir. Across the creek is a signed junction. The right fork continues on to Blackmore Lake—Hike 24. Take the left fork—the Crescent Lake Trail. Continue one mile through the forest to the north shore of Crescent Lake. The trail follows the northeast shore of the lake before heading to a pond at the southern tip of the reservoir and another junction. Head to the left on the West Shore Trail. The trail returns along the reservoir's west shore. Near the trailhead, cross over Blackmore Creek on a wooden bridge, completing the loop.

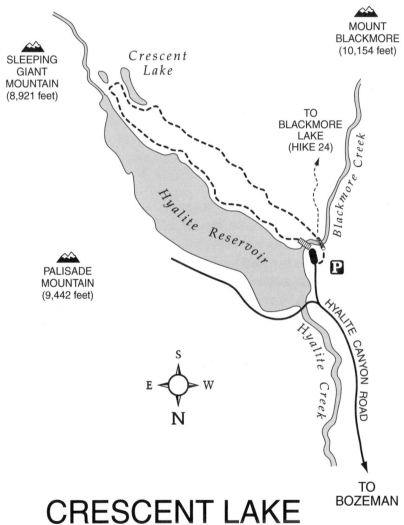

FLANDERS
MOUNTAIN
(9,961 feet)

ELEPHANT
MOUNTAIN
(10,085 feet)

MOUNT
BLACKMORE
(10,154 feet)

SLEEPING
GIANT
MOUNTAIN
(8,921 feet)

*Crescent
Lake*

TO
BLACKMORE
LAKE
(HIKE 24)

Blackmore Creek

Hyalite Reservoir

PALISADE
MOUNTAIN
(9,442 feet)

P

HYALITE CANYON ROAD

Hyalite Creek

S

E — W

N

TO
BOZEMAN

CRESCENT LAKE
AND
WEST SHORE LOOP

Hike 26
Hood Creek Trail
to Wild Horse Creek

Hiking distance: 4.6 miles round trip
Hiking time: 2 hours
Elevation gain: 900 feet
Maps: U.S.G.S. Fridley Peak
U.S.F.S. Hyalite Drainage map
Crystal Bench Maps — Bozeman, Montana

Summary of hike: The Hood Creek Trail #436 is also known as the Wild Horse Creek Trail. The trail parallels Hood Creek but the creek is never within sight or sound. The trail heads up the foothills of Palisade Mountain to great overlooks of the Hyalite Creek drainage, the East Fork of Hyalite Creek drainage, Mount Blackmore and the Hyalite Reservoir. The trail eventually leads to Mystic Lake and is also part of an 8.5-mile loop hike with the Lick Creek Road.

Driving directions: From Main Street and 19th Avenue in Bozeman, drive south on 19th Avenue, which becomes South 19th Road, 7 miles to Hyalite Canyon Road on the left—turn left. Continue 11 miles, crossing to the east side of Hyalite Reservoir to the signed "Trail 436" on the left, 20 yards south of the Hood Creek boat ramp and picnic area turnoff. Parking is not available at the trailhead, so turn right into the picnic area. Bear left at the first turn, and park in the day-use parking area by Campsite 20.

Hiking directions: Hike back up the campground road to the signed trailhead on the east side of the main road. Head uphill to the northeast through the forest, and cross an old jeep road. Wide, sweeping switchbacks weave up the hill to an overlook of Hyalite Lake and Mount Blackmore. At one mile the trail reaches an old unpaved road. Follow the road 0.1 mile to the left and leave the road, bearing right at the "trail" sign. Head uphill to an overlook of the East Fork and Main Fork of Hyalite

Creek (Hikes 28 and 30). Follow the exposed ridge uphill, reaching the shade of the forest as the trail levels out. Continue to a T-junction and bear left. At 2.3 miles, the trail crosses a gravel bridge over Wild Horse Creek. After crossing is a junction. This is our turnaround spot.

To hike further, the right fork leads several more miles to Bozeman Creek and Mystic Lake. The left fork follows the Lick Creek Road, returning to the Hyalite Canyon Road north of Hyalite Reservoir.

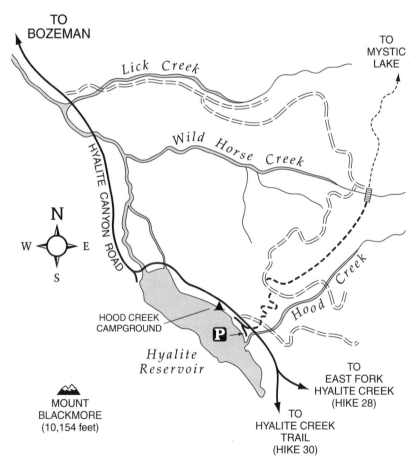

HOOD CREEK TRAIL

Hike 27
Palisade Falls

Hiking distance: 1.2 miles round trip
Hiking time: 30 minutes
Elevation gain: 250 feet
Maps: U.S.G.S. Fridley Peak
  U.S.F.S. Hyalite Drainage map
  Crystal Bench Maps — Bozeman, Montana

Summary of hike: The hike to Palisade Falls follows a paved wheelchair accessible trail. The forested trail parallels the East Fork of Hyalite Creek to a tall and beautiful waterfall on Palisade Mountain. The towering falls weaves a mosaic of white patterns cascading off the rocks below. At the trailhead is a picnic area.

Driving directions: From Main Street and 19th Avenue in Bozeman, drive south on 19th Avenue, which becomes South 19th Road, 7 miles to Hyalite Canyon Road on the left—turn left. Continue 11.7 miles, crossing to the east side of Hyalite Reservoir, to a road fork. Take the left fork one mile to the Palisade Falls parking and picnic area on the left.

Hiking directions: From the parking area, follow the paved path to the east. The trail switchbacks up to a bridge that crosses the East Fork of Hyalite Creek. From the bridge is a stunning frontal view of Palisade Falls. To return, follow the same path back.

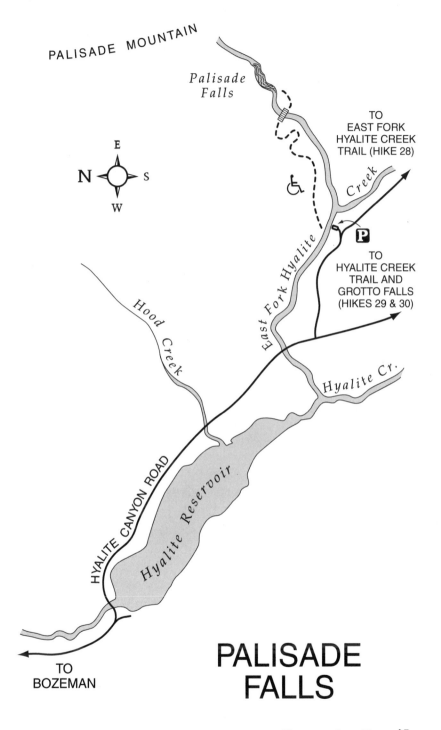

PALISADE MOUNTAIN

Palisade Falls

N E S W

TO
EAST FORK
HYALITE CREEK
TRAIL (HIKE 28)

Creek

P

TO
HYALITE CREEK
TRAIL AND
GROTTO FALLS
(HIKES 29 & 30)

East Fork Hyalite

Hood Creek

Hyalite Cr.

HYALITE CANYON ROAD

Hyalite Reservoir

TO
BOZEMAN

PALISADE
FALLS

Hike 28
East Fork Hyalite Creek Trail

Hiking distance: 10 miles round trip
Hiking time: 5 hours
Elevation gain: 2,000 feet
Maps: U.S.G.S. Fridley Peak
U.S.F.S. Hyalite Drainage map
Crystal Bench Maps — Bozeman, Montana

Summary of hike: Emerald Lake and Heather Lake sit in a high mountain alpine meadow at the head of the East Fork Hyalite Creek drainage. The towering rock walls of Mount Chisholm and Overlook Mountain drop sharply to the shore, forming a dynamic cirque around the lakes. The trail passes Horsetail Falls, a long, narrow waterfall tumbling off the west canyon wall and a 60-foot unnamed waterfall in the creek drainage.

Driving directions: From Main Street and 19th Avenue in Bozeman, drive south on 19th Avenue, which becomes South 19th Road, 7 miles to Hyalite Canyon Road on the left—turn left. Continue 11.7 miles, crossing to the east side of Hyalite Reservoir, to a road fork. Take the left fork 2.1 miles, passing the Palisade Falls parking area, to the trailhead parking lot at the end of the road.

Hiking directions: The trail heads south through the forest above the East Fork Hyalite Creek. Head up the drainage, crossing a log bridge at 0.5 miles. Horsetail Falls, a series of tall, narrow braids of water, can be seen on the west canyon wall at 1.5 miles. At 3 miles, the trail reaches the banks of the creek in a small meadow. Across the canyon are Flanders Mountain and The Mummy. Ascend the hill, zigzagging up 10 switchbacks and gaining 400 feet in a half mile. At the edge of the cliff by the second switchback is the beautiful 60-foot waterfall. At the top of the switchbacks are great views back down the canyon. The trail levels out near the base of Mount Chisholm. Cross a log bridge over the East Fork Hyalite Creek, and cross

the high open meadow with stands of conifers. Four switchbacks lead to an array of wildflowers in a second meadow.
Cross a culvert over a stream to an overlook of the lake and a
trail split. The left fork follows the northeast shoreline and
circles the lake. The right fork—the main trail—continues past
the north end of Emerald Lake, reach-
ing Heather Lake a half mile further.
The trail circles Heather Lake in
a cirque at the base of
Overlook Mountain
and Mount Chisholm.
Return by revers-
ing your route.

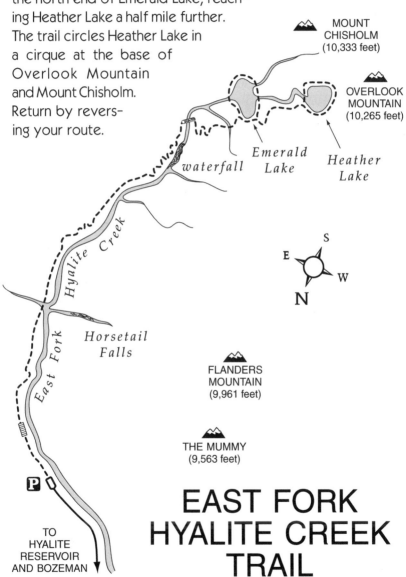

MOUNT
CHISHOLM
(10,333 feet)

OVERLOOK
MOUNTAIN
(10,265 feet)

*Emerald
Lake*

*Heather
Lake*

waterfall

Hyalite Creek

*Horsetail
Falls*

East Fork

FLANDERS
MOUNTAIN
(9,961 feet)

THE MUMMY
(9,563 feet)

P

TO
HYALITE
RESERVOIR
AND BOZEMAN

EAST FORK
HYALITE CREEK
TRAIL

Hike 29
Grotto Falls

Hiking distance: 2.5 miles round trip
Hiking time: 1.25 hours
Elevation gain: 250 feet
Maps: U.S.G.S. Fridley Peak
U.S.F.S. Hyalite Drainage map
Crystal Bench Maps — Bozeman, Montana

Summary of hike: Grotto Falls is a wide and magnificent waterfall. The forested trail to Grotto Falls is an easy wheelchair accessible gravel path. The surrounding mountains tower above the trail throughout the hike. Log benches have been placed at beautiful stopping points alongside Hyalite Creek.

Driving directions: From Main Street and 19th Avenue in Bozeman, drive south on 19th Avenue, which becomes South 19th Road, 7 miles to Hyalite Canyon Road on the left—turn left. Continue 11.7 miles, crossing to the east side of Hyalite Reservoir, to a road fork. Take the right fork 1.9 miles to the Hyalite Creek/Grotto Falls parking area at the road's end.

Hiking directions: From the parking area, hike south past the trailhead sign along the wide trail. A short distance ahead is a junction with the Hyalite Creek Trail. These two trails crisscross each other four times en route to the falls, and each junction is well marked. The Grotto Falls Trail is the wider trail and leads directly to the waterfall, where a log bench overlooks the falls. Return along the same trail.

For a longer hike, continue on the Hyalite Creek Trail (Hike 30). It leads four miles further and 1,800 feet higher to Hyalite Lake and the Hyalite Basin. The trail passes ten stairstepping waterfalls along the way.

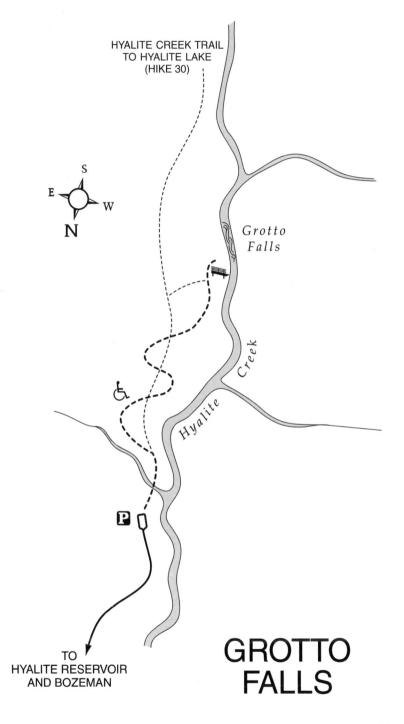

HYALITE CREEK TRAIL
TO HYALITE LAKE
(HIKE 30)

*Grotto
Falls*

Hyalite Creek

S

E ✦ W

N

P

TO
HYALITE RESERVOIR
AND BOZEMAN

GROTTO
FALLS

Hike 30
Hyalite Creek Trail to Hyalite Lake

Hiking distance: 11 miles round trip
Hiking time: 5 hours
Elevation gain: 2,000 feet
Maps: U.S.G.S. Fridley Peak, U.S.F.S. Hyalite Drainage map
Crystal Bench Maps — Bozeman, Montana

Summary of hike: The Hyalite Creek Trail is the premier hike in the entire Bozeman area. The trail passes eleven waterfalls in a deep canyon with massive cliff walls and majestic peaks. The hike ends at Hyalite Lake, a high mountain alpine lake in a horseshoe-shaped basin (back cover photo). The lake is surrounded by the craggy peaks of Fridley Peak and Hyalite Peak.

Driving directions: Follow the driving directions for Hike 29 to the Hyalite Creek/Grotto Falls parking area.

Hiking directions: The Hyalite Creek Trail heads south on a wide path through the forest. The Grotto Falls Trail (Hike 29) begins on the same path but zigzags through the forest, crossing the Hyalite Creek Trail four times. At the last junction, the left fork bypasses Grotto Falls and heads up the canyon. On the west canyon wall to the south of Elephant Mountain is Twin Falls, two waterfalls side by side plunging off the sheer cliffs. At 1.4 miles, a signed side path leads to Arch Falls on the right, a falls with a natural rock arch. At 2.2 miles, a signed detour to the left leads to Silken Skein Falls. A short distance ahead on the right is an unnamed 20-foot waterfall in a rock bowl with a pool. At 3 miles, a short detour leads to Champagne Falls, an 80-foot waterfall in a narrow fern-lined rock grotto. At 3.7 miles there are three successive waterfalls—Chasm, Shower and Apex. Cross a log footbridge over Hyalite Creek below the base of Apex Falls. Rock hop over Shower Creek (cover photo), loop back and recross the creek at a stunning cascade. Cross to the east side of Hyalite Creek and pass S'il Vous Plait Falls. Recross the creek at the base of Alpine Falls and traverse the cliff overlooking the entire U-shaped canyon to a signed junction at 5.3 miles. Bear left to a second junction. The right fork leads to Hyalite Peak, 2 miles ahead. The left fork leads 100 yards to an overlook of Hyalite Lake at the base of Fridley Peak and Hyalite Peak. Descend to the shoreline in the dramatic mountain bowl. Return on the same trail.

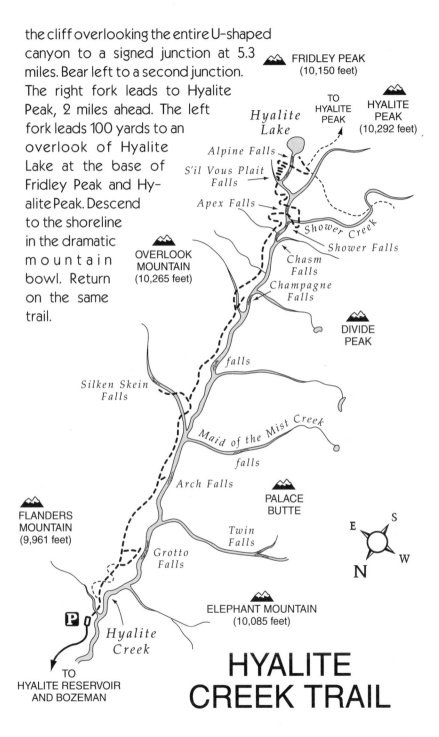

FRIDLEY PEAK
(10,150 feet)

TO HYALITE PEAK

HYALITE PEAK
(10,292 feet)

Hyalite Lake

Alpine Falls

S'il Vous Plait Falls

Apex Falls

Shower Creek

Shower Falls

OVERLOOK MOUNTAIN
(10,265 feet)

Chasm Falls

Champagne Falls

DIVIDE PEAK

falls

Silken Skein Falls

Maid of the Mist Creek

falls

Arch Falls

PALACE BUTTE

FLANDERS MOUNTAIN
(9,961 feet)

Twin Falls

Grotto Falls

E   S

N   W

ELEPHANT MOUNTAIN
(10,085 feet)

P

Hyalite Creek

TO HYALITE RESERVOIR AND BOZEMAN

HYALITE CREEK TRAIL

Hike 31
Bear Trap Canyon Trail

Hiking distance: 0.5 to 14 miles round trip
Hiking time: 30 minutes and up
Elevation gain: 50 feet to 500 feet
Maps: U.S.G.S. Bear Trap Creek, Norris, Ennis Lake
  U.S.F.S. Gallatin National Forest — West Half
  BLM Bear Trap Canyon Wilderness Guide

Summary of hike: The Bear Trap Canyon Trail, located in the Lee Metcalf Wilderness, hugs the eastern shore of the Madison River. This is a well known and popular trout fishing area. The trail winds through the 6,000-acre canyon along sheer rock cliffs carved 1,500 feet deep by the river. The only hiking access is from the north, insuring solitude the deeper into the canyon you hike. The full length of the trail is seven miles long. At the southern end is the dam and powerhouse holding back Ennis Lake. Hiking is prohibited around the dam.

Driving directions: From Bozeman, drive 9 miles west to Four Corners. Continue 20.7 miles west on Highway 84 to Bear Trap Road on the left. It is located by the Bear Trap Recreational Area sign, just before the bridge crossing the Madison River. Turn left and drive on the gravel road 3.2 miles along the east side of the river. The trailhead parking area is at the road's end.

Hiking directions: From the parking area, hike south along the east bank of the Madison River. The wide trail soon becomes a footpath and follows the eastern edge of the cliffs. At 3.5 miles Bear Trap Creek enters the Madison River from the east. There are also campsites here. You can turn around at any point, so hike as deep into the canyon as you choose. Follow the same path back.

Caution: Bear Trap Canyon has rattlesnakes. As a precaution, a snakebite kit is recommended.

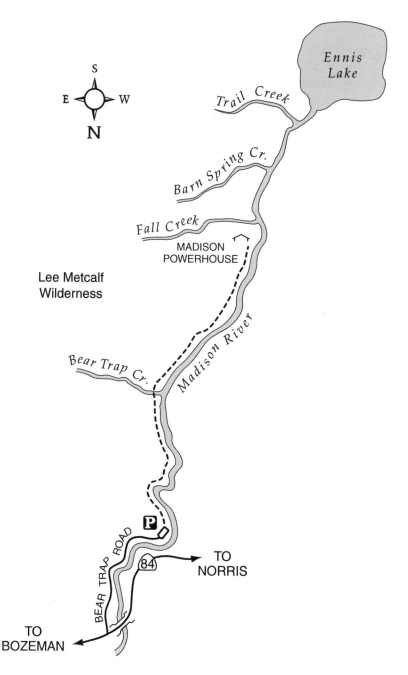

Ennis Lake

Trail Creek

Barn Spring Cr.

Fall Creek

MADISON POWERHOUSE

Lee Metcalf Wilderness

Bear Trap Cr.

Madison River

P

BEAR TRAP ROAD

84

TO NORRIS

TO BOZEMAN

S
E · W
N

BEAR TRAP CANYON

Hike 32
South Fork Trail to Pioneer Falls

Hiking distance: 7.5 miles round trip
Hiking time: 3.5 hours
Elevation gain: 800 feet
Maps: U.S.G.S. Beacon Point and Willow Swamp
Rocky Mountain Surveys Spanish Peaks

Summary of hike: The Spanish Creek Road to the trailhead is a public access road through Ted Turner's Flying D Ranch. The drive through the ranch has spectacular views. The hiking trail parallels the South Fork of Spanish Creek. Gallatin Peak, Beacon Point and Blaze Mountain are in full view high above the trail. A series of switchbacks along the Falls Creek Trail leads to the 40-foot, full-bodied Pioneer Falls.

Driving directions: From Four Corners 9 miles west of Bozeman, take Highway 191 south towards the Gallatin Canyon. Drive 13.1 miles to Spanish Creek Road on the right—turn right. Continue on Spanish Creek Road 9 miles to the Spanish Creek Campground and trailhead parking area.

From Big Sky, Spanish Creek Road is 20.7 miles north on Highway 191.

Hiking directions: From the parking area, take the trail to the west, crossing the bridge over the South Fork of Spanish Creek. Once over the river, take the trail to the left, heading upstream. At 0.3 miles, you will enter the Lee Metcalf Wilderness. The trail crosses several streams and weaves through open stands of evergreen trees while staying close to the South Fork. At 3 miles is a posted junction. Take the right fork heading up Falls Creek. The .75-mile zigzag trail rises 450 feet to Pioneer Falls. The trail leads to the brink of the falls. Shortly before reaching the top, a side trail leads to a magnificent view of the waterfall. To return, follow the same trail back.

The trail continues along the South Fork, connecting with Hell Roaring Creek (Hike 36) and North Fork Trail (Hike 39).

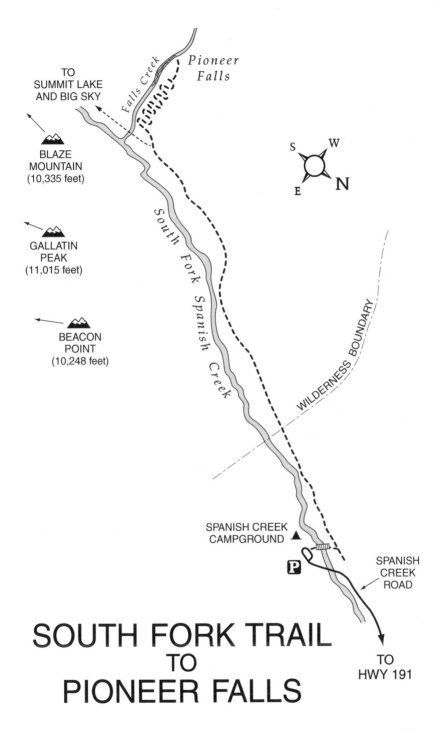

TO
SUMMIT LAKE
AND BIG SKY

Falls Creek

*Pioneer
Falls*

BLAZE
MOUNTAIN
(10,335 feet)

S W

N

E

GALLATIN
PEAK
(11,015 feet)

South Fork Spanish Creek

BEACON
POINT
(10,248 feet)

WILDERNESS BOUNDARY

SPANISH CREEK
CAMPGROUND

P

SPANISH
CREEK
ROAD

SOUTH FORK TRAIL
TO
PIONEER FALLS

TO
HWY 191

Hike 33
Gallatin Riverside Trail

Hiking distance: 5.5 miles round trip
Hiking time: 2.5 hours
Elevation gain: 200 feet
Maps: U.S.G.S. Garnet Mountain
Rocky Mountain Surveys Spanish Peaks
Crystal Bench Maps — Bozeman, Montana

Summary of hike: The Gallatin Riverside Trail parallels the eastern bank of the river. The forested trail hugs the rocky cliffs past moss-covered rocks and small streams feeding the river. Kayakers and rafters are often seen working their way downstream. This trail may be hiked one way by parking a shuttle car south of the Highway 191 bridge crossing the Gallatin River, just beyond the Lava Lake trailhead parking area.

Driving directions: From Four Corners 9 miles west of Bozeman, take Highway 191 south towards the Gallatin Canyon. Drive 16.6 miles to Squaw Creek Road (and Spire Rock Campground) on the left. Turn left, cross Squaw Creek Bridge over the Gallatin River and curve to the right. Continue 1.8 miles to the trailhead parking pullouts on both sides of the road.
From Big Sky, Squaw Creek Road is 17.2 miles north on Highway 191.

Hiking directions: The trailhead is on the south side of the road. Cross the wooden bridge over Squaw Creek. The path leads uphill 0.2 miles through the dense evergreen forest to a signed trail junction. Take the right fork, continuing on the Gallatin Riverside Trail. The trail zigzags through the forest to a grassy bench on the valley floor. A short distance ahead is a walk-through gate. From here, the trail leads to the river's edge. The trail follows the river bank along the edge of the rocky cliffs. The trail ends where the highway crosses the river. Return along the same trail.

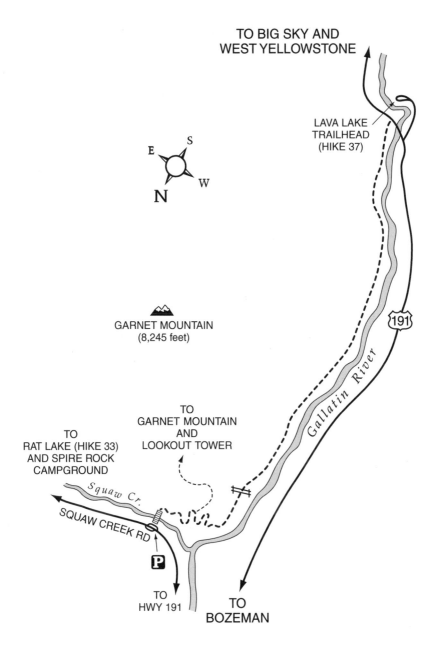

TO BIG SKY AND
WEST YELLOWSTONE

LAVA LAKE
TRAILHEAD
(HIKE 37)

S
E
N W

N

GARNET MOUNTAIN
(8,245 feet)

Gallatin River

191

TO
GARNET MOUNTAIN
AND
LOOKOUT TOWER

TO
RAT LAKE (HIKE 33)
AND SPIRE ROCK
CAMPGROUND

Squaw Cr.

SQUAW CREEK RD

P

TO
HWY 191

TO
BOZEMAN

GALLATIN
RIVERSIDE TRAIL

Hike 34
Rat Lake

Hiking distance: 1.5 miles round trip
Hiking time: 1 hour
Elevation gain: 160 feet
Maps: U.S.G.S. Garnet Mountain
Rocky Mountain Surveys Spanish Peaks

Summary of hike: Rat Lake is a beautiful lake that deserves a more attractive name. The lake, surrounded by forest, sits at 6,600 feet and is an ideal fishing, picnicking and strolling area with an accessible shoreline. The hike is short and easy, ideal for children. The beginning of the hike uses the same trail that leads 1,500 feet up to the Garnet Mountain Lookout Tower.

Driving directions: From Four Corners 9 miles west of Bozeman, take Highway 191 south towards the Gallatin Canyon. Drive 16.6 miles to Squaw Creek Road (and Spire Rock Campground) on the left. Turn left, cross Squaw Creek Bridge over the Gallatin River and curve to the right. Continue 6.7 miles to the Rat Lake trailhead parking area. Along the way are two road forks—take the right fork both times.

From Big Sky, Squaw Creek Road is 17.2 miles north on Highway 191.

Hiking directions: From the parking area, head south past the trail sign along the old jeep road. Wild lupine line the road. At 0.3 miles is a trail junction. The left fork heads up to the Garnet Mountain Lookout Tower. Take the right fork leading to the north shore of Rat Lake. At the lake, a trail loops around the wooded shoreline. After completing the loop, take the same trail back.

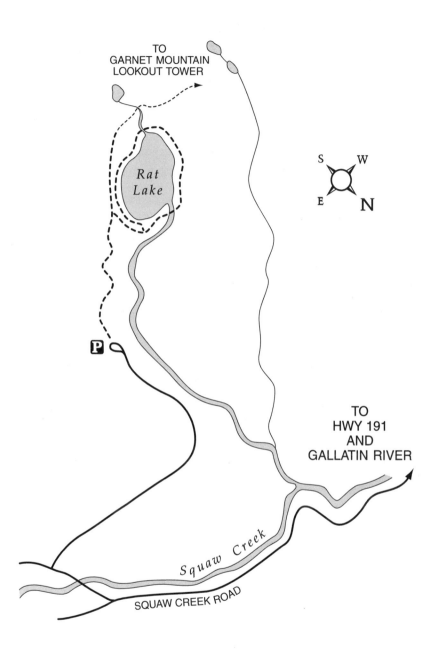

TO
GARNET MOUNTAIN
LOOKOUT TOWER

*Rat
Lake*

S W
E N

P

TO
HWY 191
AND
GALLATIN RIVER

Squaw Creek

SQUAW CREEK ROAD

RAT LAKE

Hike 35
Swan Creek Trail

Hiking distance: 1 mile to 10 miles round trip
Hiking time: 30 minutes to 5 hours
Elevation gain: 100 feet to 1,000 feet
Maps: U.S.G.S. Hidden Lake, Garnet Mountain,
Mount Blackmore, The Sentinel
Rocky Mountain Surveys Spanish Peaks
Crystal Bench Maps — Bozeman, Montana

Summary of hike: The Swan Creek Trail follows the north bank of the creek past meadows, beaver dams, volcanic rock and a pond. Swan Creek meanders through the meadows and tumbles over granite rock where the canyon narrows. The trail continues along the creek for five miles before it begins a steep ascent to 9,600 feet, where the trail connects with the Hyalite Creek Trail (Hike 30) and the Gallatin Divide Trail.

Driving directions: From Four Corners 9 miles west of Bozeman, take Highway 191 south towards the Gallatin Canyon. Drive 24.5 miles to the Swan Creek turnoff on the left. Turn left and continue 1.4 miles alongside Swan Creek to the trailhead parking area at the road's end.

From Big Sky, the Swan Creek turnoff is 9.3 miles north on Highway 191.

Hiking directions: From the parking area, the wide path heads east along the bank of Swan Creek. It quickly narrows to a footpath and enters the forest. The trail traverses the edge of the hillside overlooking Swan Creek. At 0.5 miles is a pond, then a beautiful meadow. Swan Creek winds through the meadow, pooled up by beaver dams. The trail rises and falls along the hillside, always in view of Swan Creek. Turn around at any point along this trail, making the hike as long or short as you like. Return along the same trail.

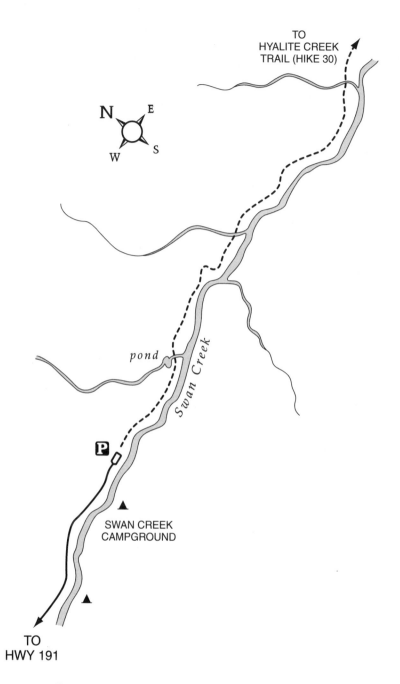

TO
HYALITE CREEK
TRAIL (HIKE 30)

N
E
S
W

pond

Swan Creek

P

SWAN CREEK
CAMPGROUND

TO
HWY 191

SWAN CREEK TRAIL

Hike 36
Hell Roaring Creek Trail

Hiking distance: 5 miles round trip
Hiking time: 2.5 hours
Elevation gain: 500 feet
Maps: U.S.G.S. Garnet Mountain and Beacon Point
U.S.F.S. Lee Metcalf Wilderness
Rocky Mountain Surveys Spanish Peaks

Summary of hike: The Hell Roaring Creek Trail, in the Lee Metcalf Wilderness, parallels Hell Roaring Creek past a continuous display of rushing, tumbling whitewater with small waterfalls, cascades and pools. The trail climbs a ridge, then crosses Hell Roaring Creek one mile from the trailhead. The Hell Roaring Creek Trail accesses a network of other trails in the Spanish Peaks.

Driving directions: From Four Corners 9 miles west of Bozeman, take Highway 191 south towards the Gallatin Canyon. Drive 18.2 miles to the Hell Roaring Creek trailhead parking area on the right.
From Big Sky, the trailhead parking area is 15.5 miles north on Highway 191.

Hiking directions: From the north end of the parking area, the trail heads southwest, entering the forest. A series of switchbacks lead 0.6 miles to a ridge. On the way up is a junction. At the junction take the hairpin switchback curving left. Once over the ridge, the trail gradually descends to Hell Roaring Creek. Cross the log bridge over the creek and head to the left up canyon. The trail continues along the north side of Hell Roaring Creek. At 2.5 miles, the trail enters the Lee Metcalf Wilderness. This is our turnaround spot.
To hike further, the trail continues up to Hell Roaring Lake, Gallatin Peak and Bear Basin.

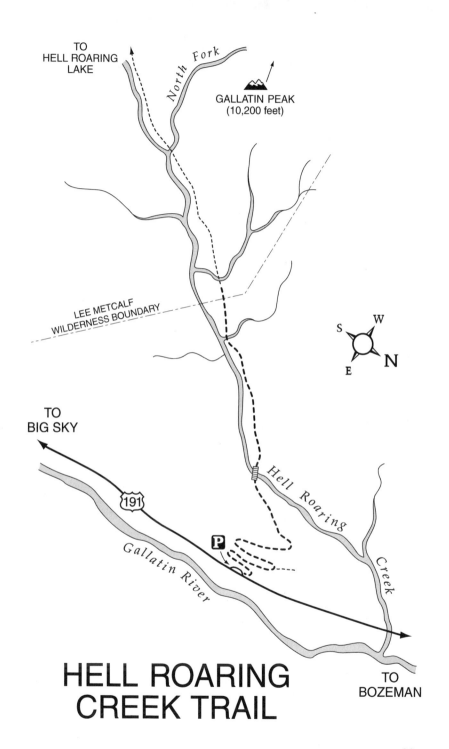

TO
HELL ROARING
LAKE

North Fork

GALLATIN PEAK
(10,200 feet)

LEE METCALF
WILDERNESS BOUNDARY

S W
N
E

TO
BIG SKY

191

Hell Roaring

P

Gallatin River

Creek

HELL ROARING
CREEK TRAIL

TO
BOZEMAN

Hike 37
Cascade Creek to Lava Lake

Hiking distance: 6 miles round trip
Hiking time: 3.5 hours
Elevation gain: 1,600 feet
Maps: U.S.G.S. Garnet Mountain and Hidden Lake
     Rocky Mountain Surveys Spanish Peaks
     Crystal Bench Maps — Bozeman, Montana

Summary of hike: The hike to Lava Lake is a steep, uphill trail through a narrow, forested canyon of pine, spruce and fir trees. The 40-acre forest-lined lake sits in a small valley surrounded by granite walls with the Spanish Peaks rising in the distance. The lake was formed by a landslide that dammed Cascade Creek. It is the only lake in the Lee Metcalf Wilderness that was not glacially formed. The trail parallels the scenic, cascading whitewater of Cascade Creek.

Driving directions: From Four Corners 9 miles west of Bozeman, take Highway 191 south towards the Gallatin Canyon. Drive 20.3 miles to the Lava Lake Trailhead parking area on the right. The turnoff is located just north of the Gallatin River bridge. Turn right and continue 0.2 miles to the parking area.

From Big Sky, the Lava Lake trailhead parking area is 13.5 miles north on Highway 191. From this direction, you can not turn left to access the trailhead parking area. Drive past to the first turnout.

Hiking directions: From the parking area, the well-marked trail heads south past the trailhead sign into the forest, immediately gaining elevation. At 0.3 miles, the trail meets Cascade Creek. The trail continues up the canyon parallel to the creek and crosses a tributary stream. At 2 miles, the trail crosses a log footbridge to the east side of Cascade Creek. The last mile is steep. The trail gains altitude with a series of switchbacks arriving at the north end of Lava Lake.

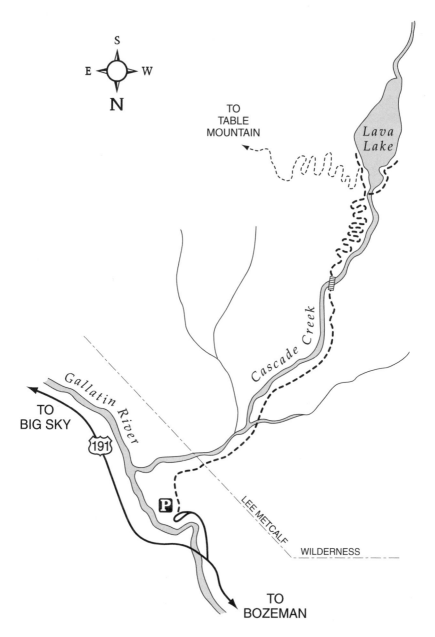

CASCADE CREEK
TO LAVA LAKE

Hike 38
Ousel Falls

Hiking distance: 1 mile round trip
Hiking time: 40 minutes
Elevation gain: 80 feet
Maps: U.S.G.S. Ousel Falls

Summary of hike: Ousel Falls is a stunning, powerful waterfall. The wide, awesome falls crashes down over the canyon walls to the narrow canyon floor. The mist created by the falls feeds the moss covering the rocks. The trail to the falls is abundant with wildflowers and has a sweeping 360-degree view of the surrounding mountains. Although there is a well-established trail to the falls, there are no trailhead signs or trail markers.

Driving directions: From Four Corners 9 miles west of Bozeman, take Highway 191 south towards the Gallatin Canyon. Drive 33.8 miles to the Big Sky turnoff on the right. Turn right and continue 2.4 miles to the unmarked Ousel Falls Road on the left. It is located directly across from Big Sky Road at the golf course. Take this unpaved road 2.1 miles to the trailhead parking area at the road's end.

Hiking directions: From the parking area, the unmarked but easily seen trail heads west. Follow the level trail 0.2 miles to a footpath leading off to the left. Take this left fork about 200 yards to another fork. Again take the left path. The forested trail follows along the canyon's edge. The cascading South Fork of the West Fork of the Gallatin River can be heard below. Watch for yet another trail to the left. This trail leads down into the canyon to Ousel Falls, which you can clearly hear. There are several trails leading down to the falls. The right fork is a gradual switchback descent. The left fork is a steeper, direct route. Return along the same trail.

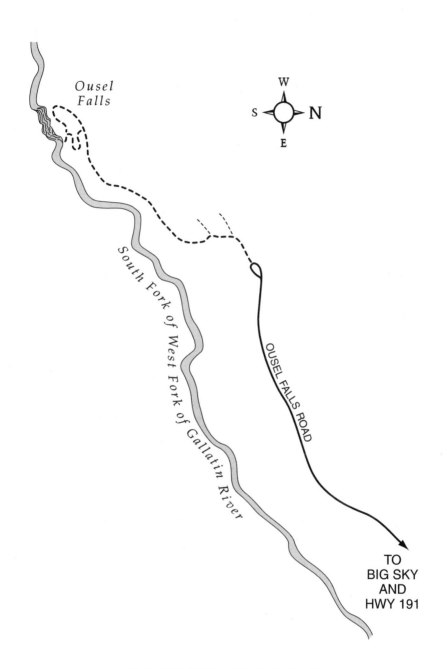

Ousel
Falls

W
S ✦ N
E

South Fork of West Fork of Gallatin River

OUSEL FALLS ROAD

TO
BIG SKY
AND
HWY 191

OUSEL FALLS

Hike 39
North Fork Trail

Hiking distance: 4 miles round trip
Hiking time: 2 hours
Elevation gain: 350 feet
Maps: U.S.G.S. Gallatin Peak
Rocky Mountain Surveys Spanish Peaks

Summary of hike: The North Fork Trail leads up to Summit Lake at an elevation of 9,500 feet. It connects with a variety of steep trails near Bear Basin, including the descent along the South Fork of Spanish Creek (Hike 32). The 16-mile North Fork—South Fork hike is a popular overnight backpack trip. This hike takes in the first two miles of the North Fork Trail. It has a gentle elevation gain and follows the beautiful open stands of evergreen trees, all within view of the North Fork.

Driving directions: From Four Corners 9 miles west of Bozeman, take Highway 191 south towards the Gallatin Canyon. Drive 33.8 miles to the Big Sky turnoff on the right. Turn right and continue 4.8 miles to the North Fork Road on the right. Turn right and drive 0.8 miles to the posted trailhead parking area.

Hiking directions: From the parking area, the wide trail heads north. The trail descends for 0.75 miles and crosses a gravel road. Continue up the canyon. The path climbs gradually but steadily. To the right is the North Fork and towering mountains, including Wilson Peak. At 2 miles, the trail crosses the North Fork. This is a great spot to spend time or picnic. Though the trail continues on the other side of the North Fork, this crossing is a good place to begin retracing your steps.

The trail continues along the North Fork to Summit Lake, 6 miles further.

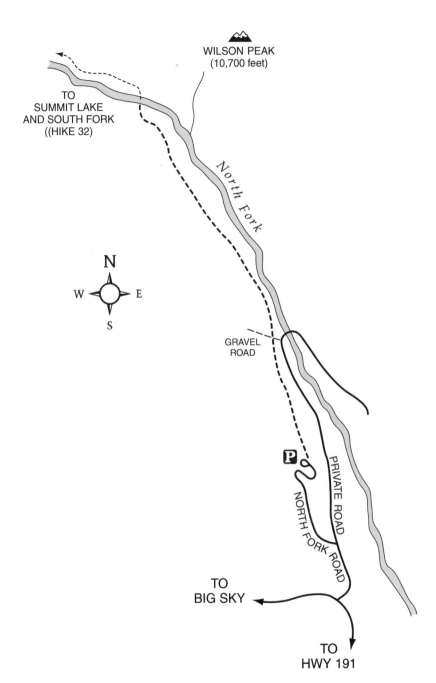

WILSON PEAK
(10,700 feet)

TO
SUMMIT LAKE
AND SOUTH FORK
((HIKE 32)

North Fork

N
W E
S

GRAVEL
ROAD

P

PRIVATE ROAD

NORTH FORK ROAD

TO
BIG SKY

TO
HWY 191

NORTH FORK TRAIL

Hike 40
Beehive Basin

Hiking distance: 4.5 miles round trip
Hiking time: 3 hours
Elevation gain: 730 feet
Maps: U.S.G.S. Lone Mountain
Rocky Mountain Surveys Spanish Peaks

Summary of hike: Beehive Basin sits in a bowl surrounded by mountains in the Spanish Peaks Primitive Area. At 9,200 feet, this top-of-the-world hike takes you to alpine meadows covered with wildflowers, tall stands of evergreens and a tributary of the Middle Fork of the Gallatin River. At the trail's end are wide open vistas and an unnamed lake.

Driving directions: From Four Corners 9 miles west of Bozeman, take Highway 191 south towards the Gallatin Canyon. Drive 33.8 miles to the Big Sky turnoff on the right. Turn right and continue 10.1 miles to the Beehive Basin turnoff on the right. (The turn is located 1.3 miles beyond the Big Sky Mountain Village turnoff and 30 yards before the Moonlight Basin Ranch entrance.) Turn right and drive on the winding road for 2.8 miles to the trailhead parking area. Park in any of the pullouts for the North Fork Tie Trail and the Ridge Trail.

Hiking directions: From the parking area, continue walking up the gravel road 0.2 miles to a sharp horseshoe bend in the road. The posted trail leads straight ahead, leaving the road behind. At 0.4 miles is a trail junction on the left. Continue straight ahead towards a large meadow and three creek crossings. After the third crossing, the trail begins its second ascent to another meadow and a pond. After crossing the second meadow, the trail begins the final ascent, then flattens out at a crescent-shaped lake in a cirque. The views are breathtaking. To return, take the same trail back.

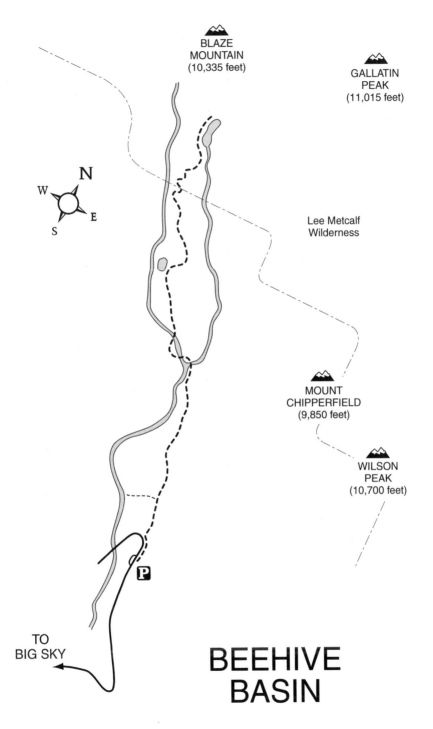

BLAZE
MOUNTAIN
(10,335 feet)

GALLATIN
PEAK
(11,015 feet)

N
W   E
S

Lee Metcalf
Wilderness

MOUNT
CHIPPERFIELD
(9,850 feet)

WILSON
PEAK
(10,700 feet)

P

TO
BIG SKY

BEEHIVE
BASIN

Hike 41
Porcupine Creek

Hiking distance: 4 miles round trip
Hiking time: 2 hours
Elevation gain: 240 feet
Maps: U.S.G.S. Lone Indian Peak

Summary of hike: The Porcupine Creek Trail follows the creek into the Porcupine Elk Preserve. The large, rolling meadows are a winter elk range. When the snow melts, moose and deer may be spotted in the meadows. The hike includes several creek crossings.

Driving directions: From Four Corners 9 miles west of Bozeman, take Highway 191 south towards the Gallatin Canyon. Drive 36.5 miles to the Porcupine Creek turnoff on the left (2.7 miles south of the Big Sky turnoff). Turn left and drive 0.5 miles, passing the log cabins, to the trailhead. Park alongside the road.

Hiking directions: The trailhead is to the left of the road. Cross the footbridge over Porcupine Creek. The wide trail heads east, parallel to the creek through open sage brush meadows dotted with pine trees. At one mile the trail crosses Porcupine Creek. To avoid getting wet feet, walk back downstream about 50 yards to a solid log crossing. Once over the creek, take the narrow footpath that rejoins the main trail. Within 50 feet is another junction. Take the left fork, and ascend the 200-foot slope. On the ridge, you can see Porcupine Creek placidly flowing through a large open meadow. The trail begins its descent into the meadow to a posted junction. This is our turnaround spot.

To hike further, take the trail to the left, crossing Porcupine Creek and the meadow. The trail heads up the ridge, crosses First Creek, then loops back. This will add two miles to the hike.

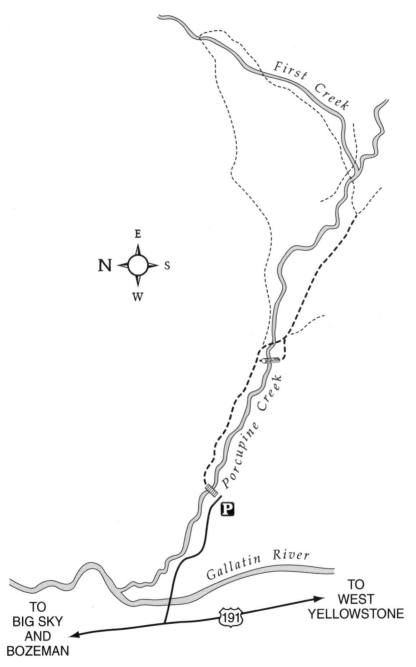

PORCUPINE CREEK

Hike 42
Tepee Creek Trail to Tepee Pass

Hiking distance: 6 miles round trip
Hiking time: 3 hours
Elevation gain: 900 feet
Maps: U.S.G.S. Sunshine Point

Summary of hike: The Tepee Creek Trail follows up the watercourse of Tepee Creek through expansive grasslands to Tepee Pass at the head of the verdant valley. From Tepee Pass are tremendous sweeping views down the wide valley and beyond, from the Madison Range to the Gallatin Range.

Driving directions: From Four Corners nine miles west of Bozeman, take Highway 191 south towards the Gallatin Canyon. Drive 49.8 miles (16 miles south of the Big Sky turnoff) to the signed trail on the left by mile marker 32. Turn left and park 100 yards ahead by the trailhead.

From West Yellowstone, the trailhead is 33 miles north on Highway 191.

Hiking directions: Head northeast up the wide grassy draw between Sunshine Point and Crown Butte. Follow the trail along Tepee Creek to a signed junction at 1.1 mile. The right fork crosses Tepee Creek and leads eastward to the park boundary (Hike 43). Take the left fork towards Tepee Pass and Buffalo Horn Divide. Climb a small hill, then traverse the hillside above the valley. Continue past Grouse Mountain and stands of aspens and pines. After numerous dips and rises along the rolling ridges, the trail begins a half-mile ascent to Tepee Pass. At the top of the valley near a stand of evergreens, there is a signed four-way junction on Tepee Pass. The right fork leads 200 yards to a flat area above the saddle with great views. This is our turnaround spot.

To hike further, the east trail leads two miles to the Yellowstone National Park boundary. From Tepee Pass, a trail descends to the north for 2.5 miles to Buffalo Horn Creek. To the west, a trail leads down Wilson Draw to the Gallatin River.

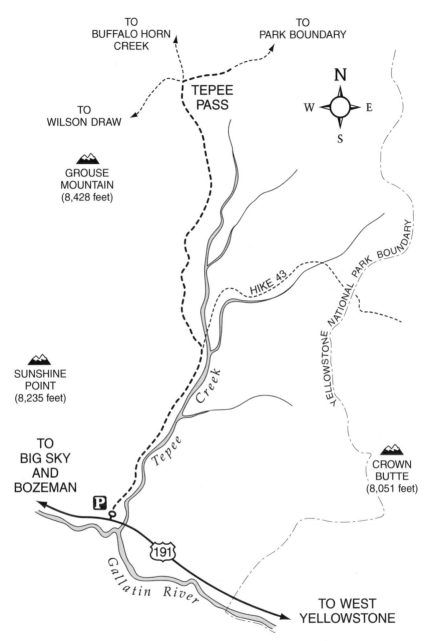

TO
BUFFALO HORN
CREEK

TO
PARK BOUNDARY

TEPEE
PASS

N
W   E
S

TO
WILSON DRAW

GROUSE
MOUNTAIN
(8,428 feet)

HIKE 43

YELLOWSTONE NATIONAL PARK BOUNDARY

SUNSHINE
POINT
(8,235 feet)

Tepee Creek

TO
BIG SKY
AND
BOZEMAN

CROWN
BUTTE
(8,051 feet)

P

191

Gallatin River

TO WEST
YELLOWSTONE

TEPEE CREEK TRAIL
TO TEPEE PASS

Hike 43
Tepee Creek Trail to the
Yellowstone National Park Boundary

Hiking distance: 4.6 miles round trip
Hiking time: 2.5 hours
Elevation gain: 700 feet
Maps: U.S.G.S. Sunshine Point

Summary of hike: The Tepee Creek Trail begins just outside the northwest corner of Yellowstone National Park. The trail crosses gentle slopes through a broad grassy valley, passing dense tree-lined ridges. The hike ends on a grassy ridgetop at the Yellowstone boundary overlooking the Daly Creek drainage.

Driving directions: From Four Corners nine miles west of Bozeman, take Highway 191 south towards the Gallatin Canyon. Drive 49.8 miles (16 miles south of the Big Sky turnoff) to the signed trail on the left by mile marker 32. Turn left and park 100 yards ahead by the trailhead.

From West Yellowstone, the trailhead is 33 miles north on Highway 191.

Hiking directions: Hike northeast past the hitching posts, and cross the grassy slopes along the base of Sunshine Point. Follow the open expanse along the west side of Tepee Creek to a signed junction at 1.1 mile. The left fork heads north to Tepee Pass and Buffalo Horn Creek (Hike 42). Take the right fork across Tepee Creek, and continue up the hillside on the east side of the creek. The trail curves to the right and heads east up a narrow drainage surrounded by mountains and tree groves. Near the top of a meadow, follow the ridge to the signed Yellowstone boundary on the saddle. Just below the saddle is a pond. Return to the trailhead the way you came.

To hike further, the trail descends into Yellowstone to Daly Creek (Hike 44).

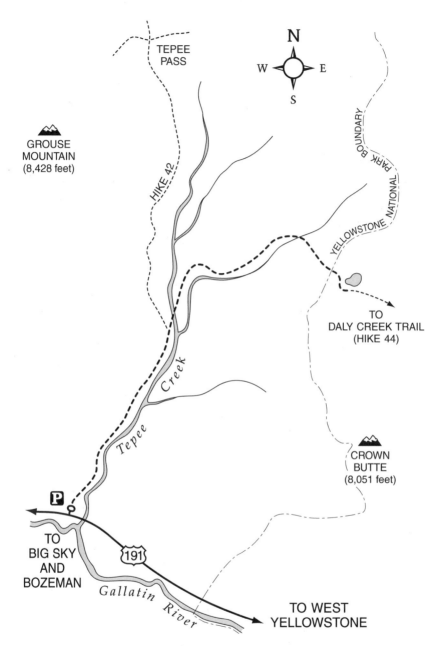

N

W   E

S

TEPEE PASS

GROUSE MOUNTAIN (8,428 feet)

HIKE 42

Tepee Creek

YELLOWSTONE NATIONAL PARK BOUNDARY

TO DALY CREEK TRAIL (HIKE 44)

CROWN BUTTE (8,051 feet)

P

TO BIG SKY AND BOZEMAN

191

Gallatin River

TO WEST YELLOWSTONE

TEPEE CREEK TRAIL
TO PARK BOUNDARY

Hike 44
Daly Creek Trail

Hiking distance: 5.2 miles round trip
Hiking time: 2.5 hours
Elevation gain: 350 feet
Maps: U.S.G.S. Sunshine Point and Big Horn Peak
      Trails Illustrated Mammoth Hot Springs

Summary of hike: Daly Creek is the northernmost drainage in Yellowstone National Park. The hike makes a gradual ascent up the scenic valley, crossing the rolling meadows and open hillsides parallel to Daly Creek. The hillsides are fringed with aspens and Douglas firs. The impressive Crown Butte, Lava Butte and King Butte formations are prominent throughout the hike. To the northeast is the Sky Rim Ridge.

Driving directions: From Four Corners nine miles west of Bozeman, take Highway 191 south towards the Gallatin Canyon. Drive 51.4 miles (17.6 miles south of the Big Sky turnoff) to the signed trail on the left between mile markers 30 and 31. Turn left and park in the lot.

From West Yellowstone, the trailhead is 31.4 miles north on Highway 191.

Hiking directions: Head northeast, skirting around the right side of the embankment parallel to Daly Creek. At a quarter mile, cross the log footbridge over Daly Creek. To the north, outside the Yellowstone Park boundary, is the Crown Butte formation. King Butte rises high in the northeast. Climb the rolling ridge along the east side of the drainage through stands of lodgepole pines. Watch for a vernal pool on the right. At one mile, the trail climbs a small hill and crosses a couple of streams to a great profile view of Crown Butte, now to the west. Continue through the open meadows past a signed junction with the Black Butte Cutoff Trail on the right at 1.8 miles. The well-defined trail reaches the Tepee Creek Cutoff Trail junction at 2.6 miles. Though the trail continues, this is a good place to begin retracing your steps.

To hike further there are two options. To the north, the trail heads up three miles further to Daly Pass at the park's northern boundary on Sky Rim Ridge. The left fork heads west into the Tepee Creek valley (Hikes 42 and 43).

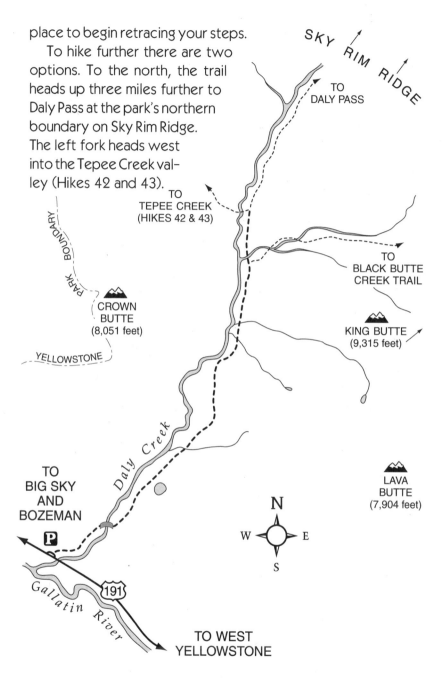

SKY RIM RIDGE

TO DALY PASS

TO TEPEE CREEK (HIKES 42 & 43)

TO BLACK BUTTE CREEK TRAIL

PARK BOUNDARY

CROWN BUTTE (8,051 feet)

YELLOWSTONE

KING BUTTE (9,315 feet)

Daly Creek

TO BIG SKY AND BOZEMAN

LAVA BUTTE (7,904 feet)

P

N
W E
S

Gallatin River

191

TO WEST YELLOWSTONE

DALY CREEK TRAIL

Hike 45
Black Butte Creek Trail

Hiking distance: 4 miles round trip
Hiking time: 2 hours
Elevation gain: 600 feet
Maps: U.S.G.S. Big Horn Peak
Trails Illustrated Mammoth Hot Springs

Summary of hike: The Black Butte Creek Trail begins just northwest of Black Butte. The trail parallels Black Butte Creek up a beautiful forested drainage to a meadow at the base of King Butte. The narrow valley has aspen, lodgepole pine and Douglas fir. This trail is an access route up to Big Horn Peak, Shelf Lake and the summit of Sheep Mountain.

Driving directions: From Four Corners nine miles west of Bozeman, take Highway 191 south towards the Gallatin Canyon. Drive 53 miles (19.2 miles south of the Big Sky turnoff) to the signed trail on the left. Park on the right, 50 yards south of the signed trail in the parking area between mile markers 28 and 29.

From West Yellowstone, the trailhead is 29.8 miles north on Highway 191.

Hiking directions: Cross the highway to the signed trail on the north edge of Black Butte Creek. Hike up the forested draw between Black Butte and Lava Butte. Head gradually uphill, following the creek through meadows and pine groves along the drainage. Meander across the rolling hills while remaining close to the creek. At 1.5 miles, the trail enters a dense, old growth lodgepole forest. After a quarter mile, the path leads to an open meadow. King Butte and Big Horn Peak tower to the northeast. At two miles in the meadow at the base of King Butte is a signed trail junction. This is the turnaround spot.

To hike further, the left fork leads 2.1 miles to Daly Creek (Hike 44). The right fork crosses the meadow along Black Butte Creek. After crossing the creek, the trail begins a steep ascent to the summit of Bighorn Peak and on to Shelf Lake.

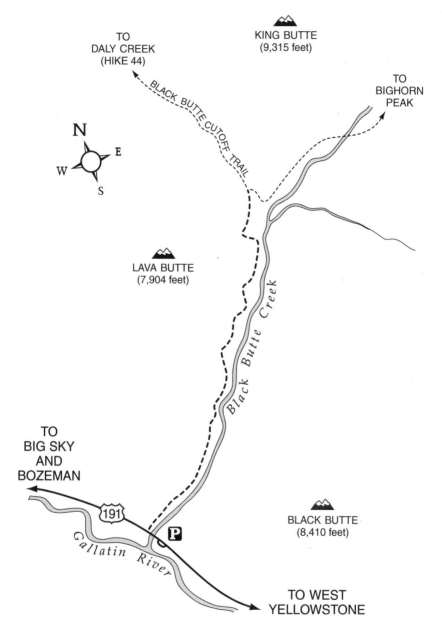

TO
DALY CREEK
(HIKE 44)

KING BUTTE
(9,315 feet)

TO
BIGHORN
PEAK

BLACK BUTTE CUTOFF TRAIL

N
W E
S

LAVA BUTTE
(7,904 feet)

Black Butte Creek

TO
BIG SKY
AND
BOZEMAN

191

Gallatin River

P

BLACK BUTTE
(8,410 feet)

TO WEST
YELLOWSTONE

BLACK BUTTE CREEK
TRAIL

Hike 46
Specimen Creek Trail

Hiking distance: 4.2 miles round trip
Hiking time: 2 hours
Elevation gain: 240 feet
Maps: U.S.G.S. Big Horn Peak
    Trails Illustrated Mammoth Hot Springs

Summary of hike: The nearly flat Specimen Creek Trail follows Specimen Creek up the canyon through a mature forest dominated by lodgepole pines. This beautiful drainage crosses bridges over feeder streams to an open meadow at the confluence of the North Fork and East Fork of Specimen Creek. The meadow is frequented by elk and moose.

Driving directions: From Four Corners nine miles west of Bozeman, take Highway 191 south towards the Gallatin Canyon. Drive 55.3 miles (21.5 miles south of the Big Sky turnoff) to the signed trail on the left between mile markers 25 and 26. Turn left and park by the trailhead 30 yards ahead.

 From West Yellowstone, the trailhead is 27.5 miles north on Highway 191.

Hiking directions: Head east parallel to Specimen Creek through the lodgepole pine forest. Pass talus slopes on the northern side of the narrow drainage. As the canyon widens, the trail alternates between stands of pines and open meadows. At 1.3 miles cross a footbridge over a stream. Traverse the forested hillside to another footbridge to a signed trail split at two miles. The right fork follows the Sportsman Lake Trail to High Lake and Sportsman Lake, 6 and 8 miles ahead. Take the Specimen Creek Trail to the left. Within minutes is Campsite WE1. The campsite sits in an open meadow by Specimen Creek. A short distance ahead is the confluence of the North Fork and the East Fork. This is our turnaround spot.

 To hike further, the trail continues up to the headwaters of the North Fork at Crescent Lake and Shelf Lake.

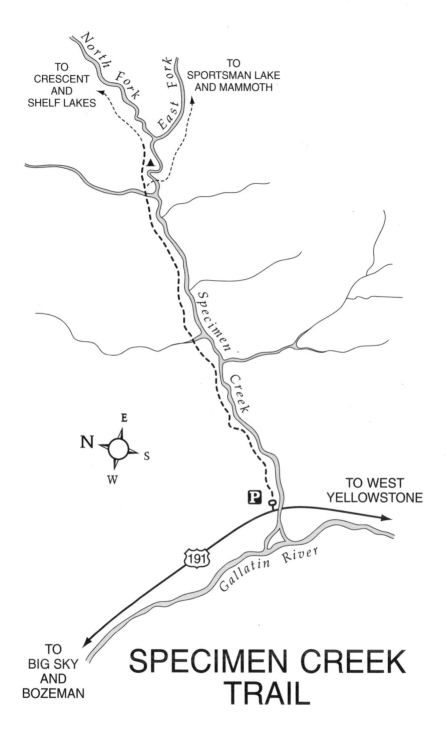

TO
CRESCENT
AND
SHELF LAKES

North Fork

East Fork

TO
SPORTSMAN LAKE
AND MAMMOTH

Specimen Creek

N E S W

P

TO WEST
YELLOWSTONE

191

Gallatin River

TO
BIG SKY
AND
BOZEMAN

SPECIMEN CREEK
TRAIL

Hike 47
Bacon Rind Creek Trail

Hiking distance: 4.2 miles round trip
Hiking time: 2 hours
Elevation gain: 200 feet
Maps: U.S.G.S. Divide Lake
      Trails Illustrated Mammoth Hot Springs

Summary of hike: The Bacon Rind Creek Trail is the only hike inside Yellowstone that heads west from the Gallatin Valley. The flat easy trail parallels the meandering Bacon Rind Creek through a valley surrounded by high mountain peaks. Moose, elk and grizzly bears frequent the meadow. Beyond the western park boundary, the trail enters the Lee Metcalf Wilderness in the Gallatin National Forest.

Driving directions: From Four Corners nine miles west of Bozeman, take Highway 191 south towards the Gallatin Canyon. Drive 59.3 miles (25.5 miles south of the Big Sky turnoff) to the trailhead sign on the right between mile markers 22 and 23. Turn right on the unpaved road 0.3 miles to the parking area.

From West Yellowstone, the trailhead is 23.5 miles north on Highway 191.

Hiking directions: Head south past the trail sign along the north side of Bacon Rind Creek. Follow the drainage upstream through beautiful stands of pines and firs. The path remains close to the riparian watercourse for the first 0.7 miles, where the valley opens up to the Gallatin River. Bacon Rind Creek flows placidly through the wide valley between the forested hillsides. Continue up the draw to the head of the valley and cross a stream. Evergreens enclose the top of the meadow at the signed Yellowstone National Park boundary. This is a good stopping place. To return, reverse route.

To hike further, the trail enters the Lee Metcalf Wilderness, crosses Migration Creek and ascends Monument Mountain.

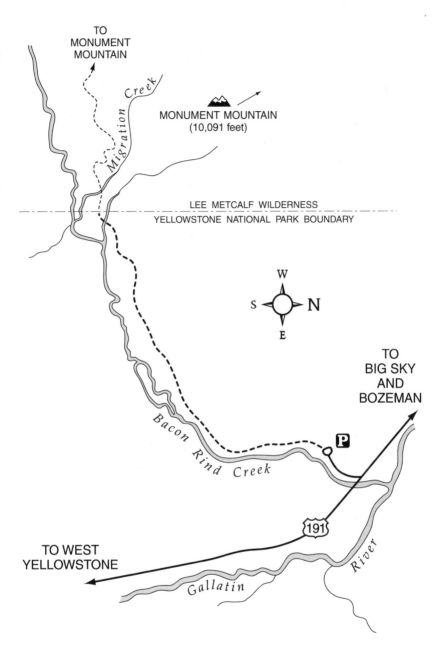

TO
MONUMENT
MOUNTAIN

Migration Creek

MONUMENT MOUNTAIN
(10,091 feet)

LEE METCALF WILDERNESS
YELLOWSTONE NATIONAL PARK BOUNDARY

W
S — N
E

TO
BIG SKY
AND
BOZEMAN

Bacon Rind Creek

P

191

TO WEST
YELLOWSTONE

River

Gallatin

BACON RIND CREEK
TRAIL

Hike 48
Fawn Pass Trail to Fan Creek

Hiking distance: 3 miles round trip
Hiking time: 1.5 hours
Elevation gain: 200 feet
Maps: U.S.G.S. Divide Lake
    Trails Illustrated Mammoth Hot Springs

Summary of hike: The Fawn Pass Trail to Fan Creek is an easy hike through forested rolling hills and scenic meadows. The Fan Creek Trail (not shown on the U.S.G.S. map) is a newer fishing access trail established in the early 1980s. From the junction with the Fawn Pass Trail, the Fan Creek Trail heads northeast along the creek through Fan Creek meadow. Moose and elk frequent this beautiful meadow.

Driving directions: From Four Corners nine miles west of Bozeman, take Highway 191 south towards the Gallatin Canyon. Drive 60 miles (26.2 miles south of the Big Sky turnoff) to the signed trail on the left, just south of mile marker 22. Turn left and park in the trailhead parking area.

From West Yellowstone, the trailhead is 22.8 miles north on Highway 191.

Hiking directions: Head east down a short flight of steps on the Fawn Pass Trail. After the trail register, cross the meadow marbled with meandering streams that make up the upper Gallatin River. A series of wooden footbridges cross the various lucid streams. Ascend the slope and enter the forested hillside. Cross the gentle rolling hills to a signed trail split at 1.4 miles. The Fawn Pass Trail bears right to the Bighorn Pass Cutoff Trail and Fawn Pass. Take the Fan Creek Trail to the left. The trail descends into the wide open meadow to Fan Creek. At the creek is a wonderful resting and picnic area.

To hike further, the trail follows Fan Creek through the mountain valley to the Sportsman Lake Trail, wading across Fan Creek three times.

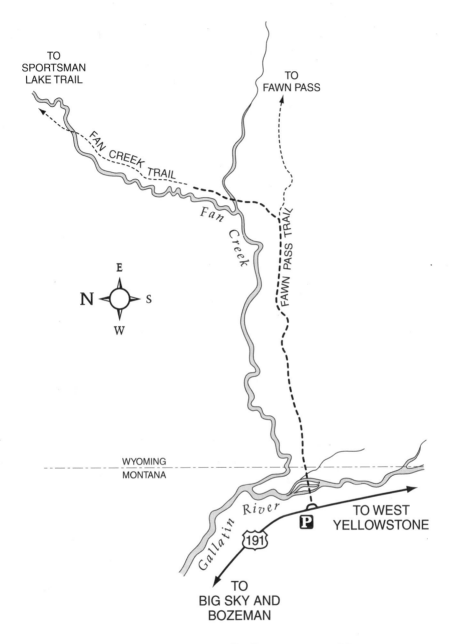

TO
SPORTSMAN
LAKE TRAIL

TO
FAWN PASS

FAN CREEK TRAIL

Fan Creek

FAWN PASS TRAIL

E

N S

W

WYOMING
MONTANA

Gallatin River

TO WEST
YELLOWSTONE

P

191

TO
BIG SKY AND
BOZEMAN

FAWN PASS TRAIL
TO FAN CREEK

Hike 49
Bighorn Pass Trail
along the Upper Gallatin River

Hiking distance: 1 to 12 miles round trip
Hiking time: Variable
Elevation gain: 150 feet
Maps: U.S.G.S. Divide Lake and Joseph Peak
        Trails Illustrated Mammoth Hot Springs

Summary of hike: The Upper Gallatin Valley is a vast, open meadow that meanders along the Upper Gallatin River for many miles. This gives you the option of choosing your own distance. The relaxing hike through the scenic, treeless valley offers excellent trout fishing and wildlife viewing. The trail eventually leads over Bighorn Pass, which can be seen looming in the distance at the end of the valley.

Driving directions: From Four Corners nine miles west of Bozeman, take Highway 191 south towards the Gallatin Canyon. Drive 61.5 miles (27.7 miles south of the Big Sky turnoff) to the signed trail on the left between mile markers 20 and 21. Turn left and drive 0.2 miles to the parking area.

From West Yellowstone, the trailhead is 21.3 miles north on Highway 191.

Hiking directions: The trail leads southeast past the hitching posts and trail sign along the west edge of the Gallatin River. Walk through the stands of lodgepole pines, heading upstream along the winding river. At a quarter mile, cross the log bridge over the river. After crossing, the trail continues southeast on the well-defined path. Follow the river through the broad grassy meadows, and enjoy spectacular views of the Gallatin Valley stretching to the east. You may turn around at any point along the trail. Bighorn Pass is 12 miles from the trailhead.

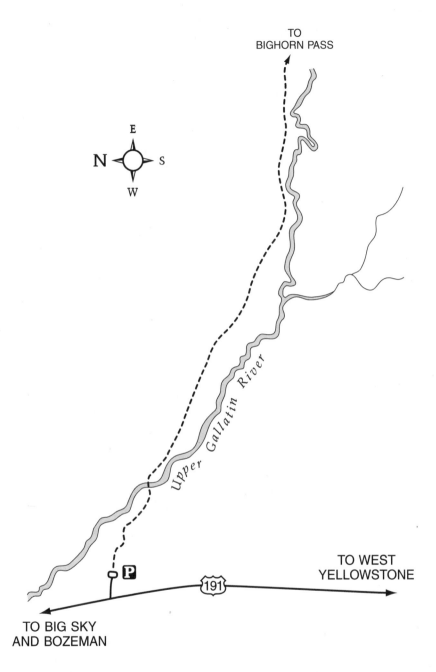

TO
BIGHORN PASS

E
N ✛ S
W

Upper Gallatin River

TO WEST
YELLOWSTONE

191

TO BIG SKY
AND BOZEMAN

BIG HORN PASS TRAIL

Hike 50
Gneiss Creek Trail from the Gallatin

Hiking distance: 3.6 miles round trip
Hiking time: 2 hours
Elevation gain: 300 feet
Maps: U.S.G.S. Richards Creek
       Trails Illustrated Mammoth Hot Springs

Summary of hike: This hike follows the first portion of the Gneiss Creek Trail from the northwest trailhead in the Gallatin. The 14-mile trail leads through the Madison Valley, crossing several creeks en route to the southern trailhead at the Madison River Bridge. This hike is an easy walk through the beautiful open terrain to Campanula Creek, a tributary of Gneiss Creek. The valley is abundant with wildlife.

Driving directions: From Four Corners nine miles west of Bozeman, take Highway 191 south towards the Gallatin Canyon. Drive 72.2 miles (38.4 miles south of the Big Sky turnoff) to the signed trail on the left between mile markers 9 and 10. Turn left and park in the area straight ahead, past Fir Ridge Cemetery.

From West Yellowstone, the trailhead is 10.6 miles north on Highway 191.

Hiking directions: Follow the old, grassy two-track road east through aspen and pine groves. Cross a small rise and parallel the signed Yellowstone Park boundary. At 0.3 miles, the trail enters the park at a sign-in register. Continue along the ridge above Duck Creek and Richards Creek to the south. Head east along the rolling hills spotted with pines and aspens. The trail gradually loses elevation past the forested slopes of Sandy Butte to the right. At the east end of Sandy Butte, descend into the draw to Campanula Creek. Follow the creek upstream a short distance to the creek crossing, the turn-around point for this hike. Return along the same path.

To hike further, cross the creek and continue southeast through the open, flat valley along Gneiss Creek.

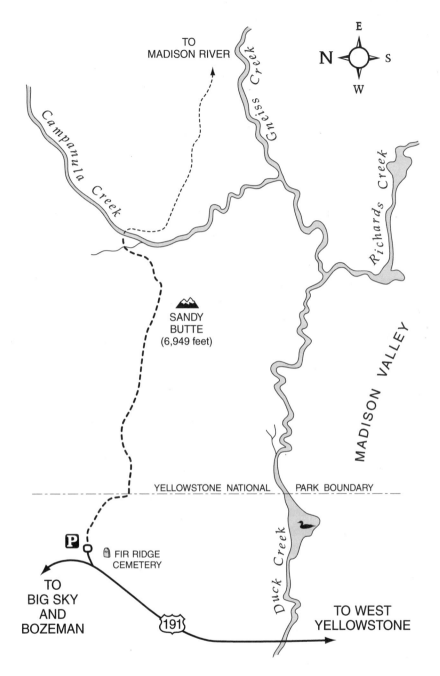

TO
MADISON RIVER

E
N ⊹ S
W

Campanula Creek

Gneiss Creek

Richards Creek

SANDY
BUTTE
(6,949 feet)

MADISON VALLEY

YELLOWSTONE NATIONAL — PARK BOUNDARY

P

FIR RIDGE
CEMETERY

Duck Creek

TO
BIG SKY
AND
BOZEMAN

191

TO WEST
YELLOWSTONE

GNEISS CREEK TRAIL

Hike 51
New World Gulch Trail

Hiking distance: 4.4 miles round trip
Hiking time: 2.5 hours
Elevation gain: 1,000 feet
Maps: U.S.G.S. Mount Ellis
U.S.F.S. Gallatin National Forest West Half or East Half
Crystal Bench Maps — Bozeman, Montana

Summary of hike: The New World Gulch Trail heads up a narrow drainage to a meadow and canyon. The area retains water, which causes muddy spots along the trail early in the season. The trail is part of a 5.5-mile loop, although the adjoining loop trail is difficult to find. This hike returns along the same trail.

Driving directions: From Bozeman, drive east on I-90 to Bear Canyon Road, the first exit east of Bozeman. Turn right on Bozeman Trail Road and continue 0.2 miles to Bear Canyon Road on the left. Turn left and drive 3.4 miles to the trailhead parking area on the right.

Hiking directions: From the parking area, hike past the buck fence up the hill. The trail leads through the forest and several stream crossings. After crossing the stream on a rickety wooden bridge, the trail enters a lodgepole pine forest and the elevation gain gets steeper. At 1.9 miles the trail descends to the gulch. A short distance ahead is the drainage stream. From the stream, take the faint trail downstream 400 yards to a beautiful, lush canyon with small waterfalls and ferns. Return to the main trail, and continue upstream 0.2 miles to a large meadow. This is our turnaround spot. To return, retrace your steps. Beyond the meadow, the trail continues on to Mystic Lake 2.5 miles further.

For the loop trail, a faint trail leads west from the meadow across the stream. Once across, the seldom used trail is a scramble to find.

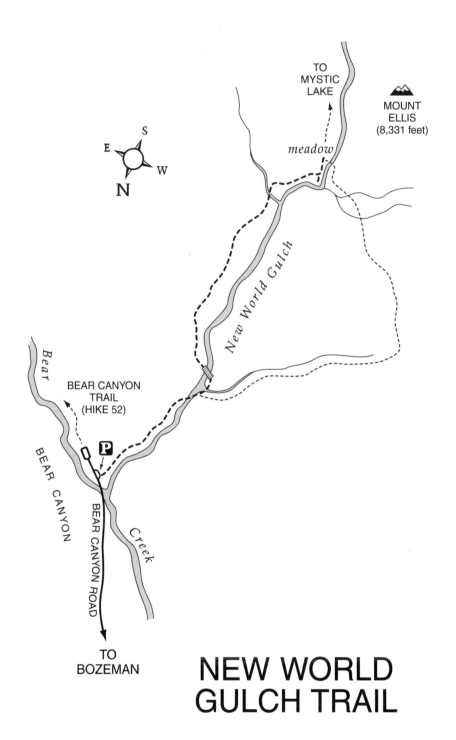

TO
MYSTIC
LAKE

MOUNT
ELLIS
(8,331 feet)

meadow

S
E W
N

New World Gulch

Bear

BEAR CANYON
TRAIL
(HIKE 52)

BEAR CANYON

P

BEAR CANYON ROAD

Creek

TO
BOZEMAN

NEW WORLD
GULCH TRAIL

Hike 52
Bear Canyon Trail

Hiking distance: 4.4 miles round trip
Hiking time: 2.5 hours
Elevation gain: 400 feet
Maps: U.S.G.S. Mount Ellis and Bald Knob
U.S.F.S. Gallatin National Forest West Half or East Half
Crystal Bench Maps — Bozeman, Montana

Summary of hike: The Bear Canyon Trail follows Bear Creek eight miles up the lush, shady canyon to the Bear Lakes. This hike takes in the first 2.2 miles of the trail, which includes several creek crossings and a one-mile loop. The trail stays close to the cascading waters of the creek. Beyond this hike, the Bear Canyon Trail climbs 1,400 feet to the Bear Lakes, which sit at an elevation of 6,900 feet.

Driving directions: From Bozeman, drive east on I-90 to Bear Canyon Road, the first exit east of Bozeman. Turn right on Bozeman Trail Road and continue 0.2 miles to Bear Canyon Road on the left. Turn left and drive 3.5 miles to the trailhead parking area at the end of the road.

Hiking directions: From the parking area, the hike begins on an old jeep road heading southeast, parallel to Bear Creek on the left. At 0.5 miles is an unsigned junction—stay to the right. (The left fork crosses Bear Creek and rejoins the trail a short distance ahead.) At 1.2 miles is a log crossing of Bear Creek. The trail passes Dean Gulch from the left. A short distance ahead is a culvert crossing over Bear Creek and a trail divide. This begins the one-mile loop. Take the right fork, which leads to a junction with the Goose Creek Trail. Stay on the main trail, bearing left to a wooden bridge crossing Bear Creek into a meadow. Two hundred feet ahead, a trail heads off to the left. The main trail through the meadow leads to Bear Lakes. Take the left fork, completing the loop, and head back to the trailhead.

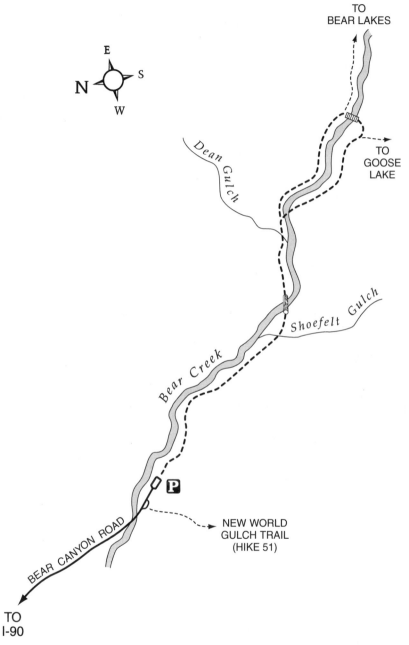

TO
BEAR LAKES

E
N ─◇─ S
W

TO
GOOSE
LAKE

Dean Gulch

Shoefelt Gulch

Bear Creek

P

NEW WORLD
GULCH TRAIL
(HIKE 51)

BEAR CANYON ROAD

TO
I-90

BEAR CANYON TRAIL

Hike 53
Pine Creek Falls

Hiking distance: 2 miles round trip
Hiking time: 1 hour
Elevation gain: 350 feet
Maps: U.S.G.S. Dexter Point and Mount Cowen
U.S.F.S. Gallatin National Forest West Half or East Half
Rocky Mountain Surveys Mt. Cowen Area

Summary of hike: The trail to Pine Creek Falls is located in the Absaroka-Beartooth Wilderness. The trail follows Pine Creek upstream to the falls through a spruce, fir, aspen and maple forest. When the creek is out of view, it can still be heard cascading downstream. Pine Creek Falls is a tall, narrow waterfall that spreads out as it plunges over rock outcroppings. It is a great place to spend some time and have a picnic lunch.

Driving directions: From Livingston at the I-90 and Highway 89 junction, drive 9.6 miles south on Highway 89 to Pine Creek Road (Highway 540) on the left. Turn left, cross the Yellowstone River, and continue 2.4 miles to East River Road. Turn right and drive 0.7 miles to Luccock Park Road on the left. A sign is posted for the Pine Creek Campground. Turn left and drive 3.1 miles on the paved road to the trailhead parking area at road's end.

Pine Creek Road is 12.3 miles north of Emigrant and 42 miles north of Gardiner.

Hiking directions: From the parking area, the well-posted trailhead is at the far end of the lot. The trail immediately enters a deep, lush forest to a junction. Take the right fork, the Pine Creek Trail. A short distance ahead is a junction with the George Lake Trail. Stay to the left. At 0.5 miles, the trail crosses over to the north side of Pine Creek via a wooden bridge. At one mile is a second wooden bridge over Pine Creek. From the bridge is a dynamic view of Pine Creek Falls. Thirty yards beyond the bridge is a side shoot of the waterfall. Several unmaintained trails offer access to the upper chute of the falls. Although this is our turnaround spot, the trail continues to Pine Creek Lake, 4 miles ahead and 3,000 feet up. Return by retracing your steps.

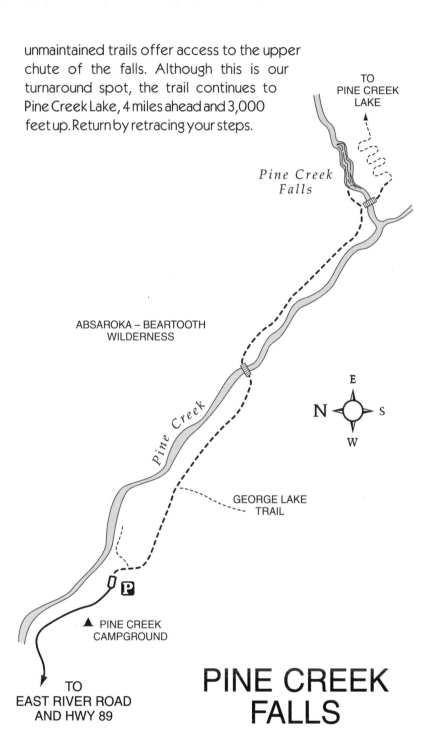

Hike 54
Passage Falls

Hiking distance: 4.2 miles round trip
Hiking time: 2.5 hours
Elevation gain: 480 feet
Maps: U.S.G.S. Knowles Peak, The Pyramid, Mount Wallace
U.S.F.S. Gallatin National Forest East Half

Summary of hike: Passage Falls is a massive, powerful waterfall that leaps over moss-covered rocks straight down to the narrow canyon's rocky floor. The trail to Passage Falls parallels Passage Creek. A side trail branches off to see the falls. The Wallace Creek Trail and Passage Creek Trail take off together as the same trail but separate upstream.

Driving directions: From Livingston at the I-90 and Highway 89 junction, drive 15.7 miles south on Highway 89 to Mill Creek Road on the left. Turn left and drive 14 miles up Mill Creek Road to the Wallace Creek trailhead parking area on the right.

Mill Creek Road is 6.2 miles north of Emigrant and 36 miles north of Gardiner.

Hiking directions: The trail begins at the bridge where Mill Creek and Passage Creek join together. Once over Mill Creek, continue south to another wooden bridge crossing over Passage Creek. At one mile the trail crosses a stream with a small waterfall and cascade. After a second stream, the forested trail emerges into a small meadow, then ducks back into the forest canopy. At 1.6 miles the path forks. Take the right branch leading to Passage Falls. Climb up the short, steep hill to a slope. From the slope are views overlooking a large meadow on private land. Take the trail to the left, and descend the eight switchbacks to Passage Falls. Return by retracing your steps.

Trails continue along Wallace Creek and Passage Creek, joining with a network of other trails.

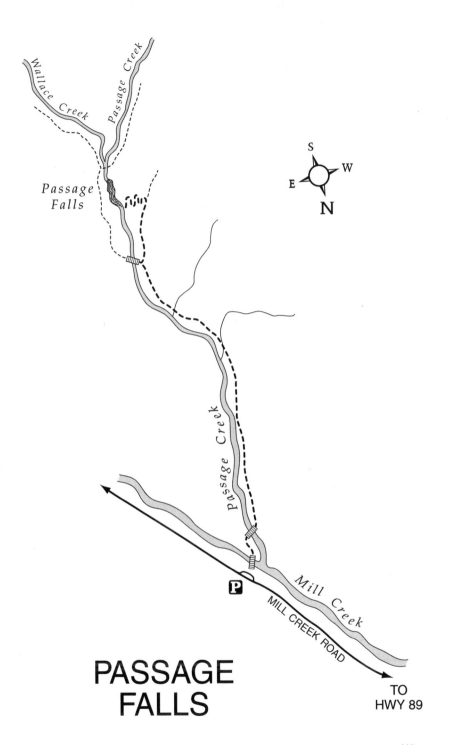

Wallace Creek

Passage Creek

S
E W
N

Passage
Falls

Passage Creek

Mill Creek

P

MILL CREEK ROAD

PASSAGE
FALLS

TO
HWY 89

Hike 55
Big Creek Trail

Hiking distance: 4 miles round trip
Hiking time: 2 hours
Elevation gain: 200 feet
Maps: U.S.G.S. Lewis Creek
U.S.F.S. Gallatin National Forest East Half

Summary of hike: The Big Creek Trail follows Big Creek to the west, providing access to a network of trails, lakes and mountain peaks. The trail heads six miles up to Windy Pass. This hike takes in the first two miles of the trail. The trail passes meadows, rock cliffs and talus slides. The trailhead is where the Big Creek Road originally crossed Big Creek. The bridge washed out, making this the end of the road and the new trailhead.

Driving directions: From Livingston at the I-90 and Highway 89 junction, drive 28.6 miles south on Highway 89 to the Big Creek Road on the right between mile markers 24 and 25. Turn right and continue 4.8 miles to the trailhead parking area at the road's end. It is located across the road from Mountain Sky Guest Ranch. (At 3.5 miles is a road fork—stay to the left.)
Big Creek road is 6.7 miles south of Emigrant and 23 miles north of Gardiner.

Hiking directions: From the parking area, hike west to the bridge crossing Big Creek. Bear to the right and pass the cattleguard. At 0.2 miles is the Forest Service guard station. Three hundred feet after the second bridge is the old trailhead information board, a short hill and the Big Creek Trail footpath. Along the trail, several side paths lead down to the meadows and Big Creek on the left. The Big Creek Trail stays on the forested mountain slope, slowly descending to a log bridge crossing over Cliff Creek at 2 miles. This is the turnaround spot.
The trail continues 4 miles further to Windy Pass and a network of other trails, closely following Big Creek.

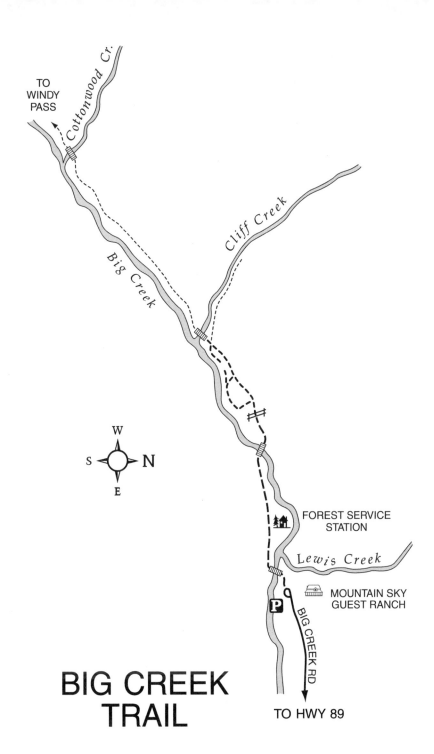

TO
WINDY
PASS

Cottonwood Cr.

Cliff Creek

Big Creek

W
S — N
E

FOREST SERVICE
STATION

Lewis Creek

MOUNTAIN SKY
GUEST RANCH

P

BIG CREEK RD

TO HWY 89

BIG CREEK
TRAIL

Hike 56
Petrified Forest Interpretive Trail

Hiking distance: 2 miles round trip
Hiking time: 1 hour
Elevation gain: 600 feet
Maps: U.S.G.S. Ramshorn Peak
U.S.F.S. Gallatin National Forest East Half

Summary of hike: The Petrified Forest Interpretive Trail begins at the west end of Tom Miner Campground. The trail leads to a line of sculpted volcanic cliffs and caves with petrified tree and fossil remains. In one cave, a petrified tree protrudes from the ceiling. From the cliffs are awesome views up and down the Trail Creek drainage.

Driving directions: From Livingston at the I-90 and Highway 89 junction, drive 37 miles south on Highway 89 to the signed Tom Miner Basin turnoff, between mile markers 16 and 17. Drive 0.4 miles on Tom Miner Creek Road, crossing a bridge over the Yellowstone River to a junction. Go left, staying on the Tom Miner Creek Road. At 8.1 miles, follow the campground sign, bearing left at a road fork. The B-Bar Ranch bears right. Continue on the narrow road to a road split at 11 miles. Curve right, entering the Tom Miner Campground. Drive to the upper (west) end of the campground to the signed trailhead at 11.7 miles. A campground parking fee is required.

The Tom Miner Basin turnoff is 15 miles south of Emigrant and 16 miles north of Gardiner.

Hiking directions: Head up the gentle grassy slope on the north side of Trail Creek through groves of aspens, spruce and pines. At a quarter mile is a signed junction. The left fork heads west up to Buffalo Horn Pass (Hike 57). Take the right fork up the meadow on the west side of a dry, rocky creekbed. Continue northwest beneath the extraordinary lava rock formations and caves. The trail leads uphill through the forest past massive lava rocks. Switchbacks lead up the south-facing mountain, reaching the sculpted cliffs and caves seen from below. Each cave has interpretive stations explaining the geology of the surroundings. After exploring the area, return by retracing your steps.

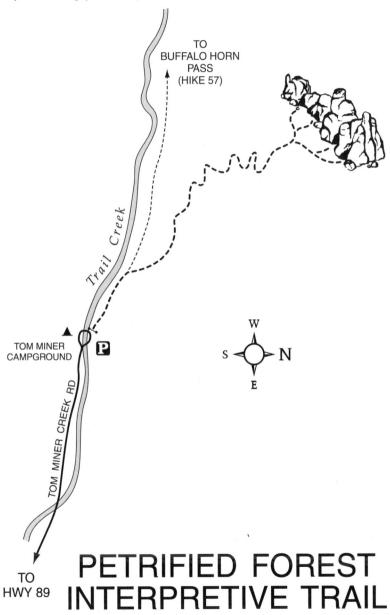

TO
BUFFALO HORN
PASS
(HIKE 57)

Trail Creek

TOM MINER
CAMPGROUND

P

TOM MINER CREEK RD

TO
HWY 89

W

S — N

E

PETRIFIED FOREST
INTERPRETIVE TRAIL

Hike 57
Buffalo Horn Pass
from Tom Miner Campground

Hiking distance: 4.6 miles round trip
Hiking time: 2.5 hours
Elevation gain: 1,450 feet
Maps: U.S.G.S. Ramshorn Peak
      U.S.F.S. Gallatin National Forest East Half

Summary of hike: The trail to Buffalo Horn Pass begins at the upper (west) end of Tom Miner Campground. The trail parallels Trail Creek past its headwaters to the round meadow at the 8,523-foot summit. Near the pass is the Gallatin Petrified Forest and a network of trails heading in every direction.

Driving directions: Follow the driving directions for Hike 56 to the Tom Miner Campground.

Hiking directions: Head west through the trailhead gate and up the grassy meadow fringed with aspen and spruce trees, paralleling Trail Creek. At a quarter mile, cross a dry streambed to a signed junction with the Petrified Forest Interpretive Trail (Hike 56). Bear to the left, heading west up the sloping meadow. Traverse the edge of the hillside above the creek, alternating between shady forest and open meadows. To the east are great views of the majestic peaks of the Absaroka Range. At 0.8 miles, rock-hop across Dry Creek and begin a steep quarter-mile ascent. The path remains on the north side of Trail Creek. At two miles, curve around the bowl at the Trail Creek headwaters, reaching the meadow at Buffalo Horn Pass. At the pass is a four-way junction, the turnaround spot for this hike.

To hike further, the left fork heads south to Yellowstone National Park. The right fork heads north to Ramshorn Peak at 10,296-feet. The west route, straight ahead, leads to Buffalo Horn Creek and follows it to the Gallatin River. Return along the same path.

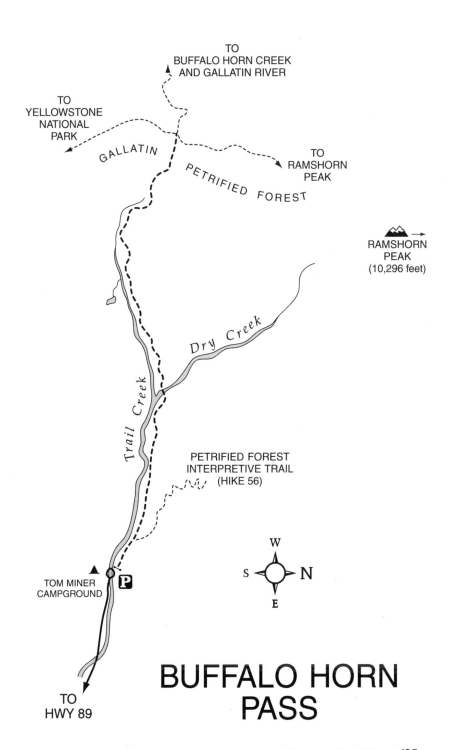

TO
BUFFALO HORN CREEK
AND GALLATIN RIVER

TO
YELLOWSTONE
NATIONAL
PARK

GALLATIN

PETRIFIED FOREST

TO
RAMSHORN
PEAK

RAMSHORN
PEAK
(10,296 feet)

Dry Creek

Trail Creek

PETRIFIED FOREST
INTERPRETIVE TRAIL
(HIKE 56)

TOM MINER
CAMPGROUND

P

W
S — N
E

BUFFALO HORN
PASS

TO
HWY 89

Other Day Hike Guidebooks

These books may be purchased at your local bookstore or outdoor shop. Or, order them direct from the distributor:

The Globe Pequot Press
246 Goose Lane · P.O. Box 480 · Guilford, CT 06437-0480
www.globe-pequot.com
800-243-0495

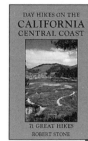

DAY HIKES ON THE
CALIFORNIA
CENTRAL COAST

71 GREAT HIKES
ROBERT STONE

DAY HIKES AROUND
**MONTEREY
& CARMEL**

77 GREAT HIKES
ROBERT STONE

DAY HIKES AROUND
BIG SUR

80 GREAT HIKES
ROBERT STONE

DAY HIKES IN
**SAN LUIS OBISPO
COUNTY**
CALIFORNIA

ROBERT STONE

DAY HIKES AROUND
**SANTA
BARBARA**

82 GREAT HIKES
ROBERT STONE

DAY HIKES IN
YOSEMITE
NATIONAL PARK

55 GREAT HIKES
ROBERT STONE

DAY HIKES IN
SEQUOIA
AND
KINGS CANYON
NATIONAL PARKS

ROBERT STONE

DAY HIKES AROUND
**VENTURA
COUNTY**

82 GREAT HIKES
ROBERT STONE

DAY HIKES AROUND
LOS ANGELES

83 GREAT HIKES
ROBERT STONE

DAY HIKES AROUND
**LAKE
TAHOE**

ROBERT STONE

DAY HIKES IN
YELLOWSTONE
NATIONAL PARK

54 GREAT HIKES
ROBERT STONE

DAY HIKES IN
**GRAND TETON
NATIONAL PARK**
AND
JACKSON HOLE

ROBERT STONE

DAY HIKES IN THE
**BEARTOOTH
MOUNTAINS**

RED LODGE, MONTANA TO
YELLOWSTONE NATIONAL PARK
ROBERT STONE

DAY HIKES AROUND
BOZEMAN
MONTANA

INCLUDING THE GALLATIN
CANYON AND PARADISE VALLEY
ROBERT STONE

DAY HIKES AROUND
MISSOULA
MONTANA

INCLUDING THE BITTERROOTS
AND THE SEELEY-SWAN VALLEY
ROBERT STONE

DAY HIKES ON
OAHU

57 GREAT HIKES
ROBERT STONE

DAY HIKES ON
MAUI

55 GREAT HIKES
ROBERT STONE

DAY HIKES ON
KAUAI

55 GREAT HIKES
ROBERT STONE

DAY TRIPS ON
ST. MARTIN

ROBERT STONE

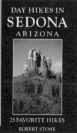

DAY HIKES IN
SEDONA
ARIZONA

25 FAVORITE HIKES
ROBERT STONE

Notes